VOGUE KNITTING
CROCHETED
SCARVES TWO

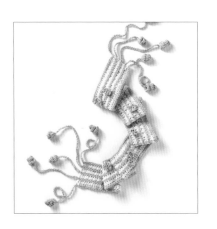

VOGUE® KNITTING

CROCHETED
SCARVES TWO

SIXTH&SPRING BOOKS
NEW YORK

SIXTH&SPRING BOOKS
233 Spring Street
New York, New York 10013

Library of Congress Cataloging-in-Publication Data

Library of Congress Control Number: 2006924840
ISBN: 1-933027-03-7
ISBN-13: 978-1-933027-03-6

Manufactured in China

1 3 5 7 9 10 8 6 4 2

First Edition
2006

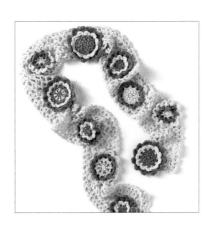

TABLE OF CONTENTS

INTRODUCTION

Fast and easy to make, scarves are the perfect accessory for any outfit. Crocheting a scarf is also a great way to relax and gain a sense of accomplishment. Think how great you will feel knowing you're creating something gorgeous and fashionable, especially if your time for creative endeavors is limited. *Crocheted Scarves Two* highlights a diverse collection of exciting designs for crocheters of all skill levels.

The patterns in *Crocheted Scarves Two* showcase a spectrum of striking colors in a wide variety of fabrics, including mohair, cotton, merino wool, and silk. A wealth of styles from cultures all over the globe are featured, including designs evocative of North Africa, Mexico, the Mediterranean, the Swiss Alps, and the Great Plains of America. Crochet enthusiasts will also enjoy the diversity of stitches used—from Tunisian crochet to mesh stitch to spike stitch—as well as a variety of whimsical floral designs.

This stylish collection gives a nod to the classics without neglecting current trends. There's a scarf for every occasion and personality here, from an attention-grabbing faux boa to a traditional basketweave design to a playful penguin scarf for the young (and young at heart).

So grab your hook, pick out some yarn to match your favorite outfit (or ten), and get ready to **CROCHET ON THE GO!**

THE BASICS

While many crafters consider crochet a family tradition, few may realize that it is a practice dating back to ancient times. Shepherds were probably the first to crochet, using hooked sticks to turn their spun wool scraps into clothes. By the sixteenth century, Irish nuns were using bone and ivory hooks to create lace patterns that crocheters still use today. And in the nineteenth century, the aspirational middle classes learned the craft in imitation of society's elite, who were educated in such handwork. So crochet became part of popular culture, a practical and artistic craft that anyone could do.

Lately, word is that crochet has made a comeback; history, though, tells us it never really left. People are just exploring new hobbies, rediscovering old skills, and expanding their knowledge of handcrafts. Our aim is to encourage and entice a whole spectrum of crocheters, whatever their experience, with this book.

Crochet is accessible and really quite easy to learn. Stitches are formed by pulling loops through other loops, or stitches, with a hook, creating the simple chain that is used in all patterns. Unlike knitting, there is no balancing act with needles, shifting stitches from one needle to another. In crochet, one hand and one hook do all the work, and finished fabric lays away from the hook, letting crocheters concentrate on only the next stitch they need to make. And, unlike other crafts, correcting a mistake is fairly stress-free—simply tug on the yarn to easily pull out the stitches you have worked.

If you're not convinced that it's easy to learn to crochet, perhaps the scarves in this collection will inspire you. They run the gamut from basic to more complicated stitches, giving experienced crocheters ample challenge and offering novices the chance to graduate to more difficult projects as they progress. The beginner scarf styles, such as the Easy Scarf on page 28 and the Cluster Stitch Fiesta Scarf on page 18, often have a simple one-row repeat and work up quickly with a very large hook and bulky weight yarn. Such basic patterns let the yarn take center stage. Meanwhile, the more advanced designs, like the Modular Scarf on page 74 and the Shell Scarf/Wrap on page 88, do not necessarily have more difficult stitch techniques; rather the instructions, with their series of repeats and pattern layouts, require more concentration to create the perfect piece.

In crochet, finished pieces have unique characteristics. The combination of chains and joining in crochet creates a sheer netting, whose airiness can dress up an outfit or just add a dash of style. Other times, the depth of the garment, depending on the chosen yarn, can actually take on a rich three-dimensional appearance. And it is just as easy to learn to finish crochet. Though crocheted pieces often lack stretchability, again, depending on the yarn used, they usually lay flat without further blocking or finishing.

We hope that by now you are eager to pick up a hook and start to crochet. If not, take a look at the pieces in this dynamic collection; in no time you will be exploring and enjoying the fresh, contemporary styles that have emerged from an ancient tradition.

YARN SELECTION

For an exact reproduction of the scarf photographed, use the yarn listed in the materials section of the pattern. We've selected yarns that are readily available in the U.S. and Canada at the time of printing. The Resources list on page 94 provides addresses of yarn distributors. Contact them for the name of a retailer in your area.

CROCHET HOOKS					
U.S.	**Metric**	**U.S.**	**Metric**	**U.S.**	**Metric**
B/1	2.25mm	G/6	4mm	K/10.5	6.5mm
C/2	2.75mm	7	4.5mm	L/11	8mm
D/3	3.25mm	H/8	5mm	M/13	9mm
E/4	3.5mm	I/9	5.5mm	N/15	10mm
F/5	3.75mm	J/10	6mm		

You may wish to substitute yarns. Perhaps a spectacular yarn matches your new coat; maybe you view small-scale projects as a chance to incorporate leftovers from your yarn stash; or it may be that the yarn specified is not available in your area. Scarves allow you to be as creative as you like, but you'll need to crochet to the given gauge to obtain the finished measurements with the substitute yarn. Make pattern adjustments where necessary. Be sure to consider how different yarn types (chenille, mohair, bouclé, etc.) will affect the final appearance of your scarf, and how they will feel against your skin. Also take fiber care into consideration: Some yarns can be machine- or hand-washed; others will require dry cleaning.

To facilitate yarn substitution, *Vogue Knitting* grades yarn by the standard stitch gauge obtained in single crochet. You'll find a grading number in the "Materials" section of the pattern, immediately following the yarn information. Look for a substitute yarn that falls into the same category. The suggested hook size and gauge on the ball band should be comparable to that on the Standard Yarn Weight chart at right.

After you've successfully gauge-swatched a substitute yarn, you'll need to determine how much of the substitute yarn the project requires. First, find the total yardage of the original yarn in the pattern (multiply the number of balls by yards/meters per ball). Divide this figure by the new yards/meters per ball (listed on the ball band). Round up to the next whole number. The result is the number of balls required.

READING CROCHET INSTRUCTIONS

If you are used to reading knitting instructions, then crochet instructions may seem a little tedious to follow. Crochet instructions use more abbreviations and punctuation and fewer words than traditional knitting instructions. Along with the separation of stitches and use of brackets, parentheses, commas, and other punctuation, numerous repetitions may occur within a single row or round. Therefore, you must pay close attention to reading instructions while you crochet. Here are a few explanations of the more common terms used in this book.

Use of Parentheses ( )

Sometimes parentheses are used to indicate stitches that are to be worked all into one stitch such as "in next st work ( )" or "( ) in next st."

First st, Next st

The beginning stitch of every row is referred to as the "first st." When counting the turning chain (t-ch) as one stitch, the

Categories of yarn, gauge ranges, and recommended needle and hook sizes

Yarn Weight Symbol & Category Names	⓵ Super Fine	⓶ Fine	⓷ Light	⓸ Medium	⓹ Bulky	⓺ Super Bulky
Type of Yarns in Category	Sock, Fingering, Baby	Sport, Baby	DK, Light Worsted	Worsted, Afghan, Aran	Chunky, Craft, Rug	Bulky, Roving
Knit Gauge Range* in Stockinette Stitch to 4 Inches	27–32 sts	23–26 sts	21–24 sts	16–20 sts	12–15 sts	6–11 sts
Recommended Needle in Metric Size Range	2.25–3.25 mm	3.25–3.75 mm	3.75–4.5 mm	4.5–5.5 mm	5.5–8 mm	8 mm and larger
Recommended Needle U.S. Size Range	1 to 3	3 to 5	5 to 7	7 to 9	9 to 11	11 and larger
Crochet Gauge* Ranges in Single Crochet To 4 Inch	21–32 sts	16–20 sts	12–17 sts	11–14 sts	8–11 sts	5–9 sts
Recommended Hook in Metric Size Range	2.25–3.5 mm	3.5–4.5 mm	4.5–5.5 mm	5.5–6.5 mm	6.5–9 mm	9 mm and larger
Recommended Hook U.S. Size Range	B–1 to E–4	E–4 to 7	7 to I–9	I–9 to K–10½	K–10½ to M–13	M–13 and larger

*Guidelines only: The above reflects the most commonly used needle or hook sizes for specific yarn categories.

Beginner

Ideal first project.

Very Easy Very Vogue

Basic stitches, minimal shaping, simple finishing.

Intermediate

For crocheters with some experience. More intricate stitches, shaping and finishing.

Experienced

For crocheters able to work patterns with complicated shaping and finishing.

row or round will begin by instructing that you work into the next st (that is, skip the first st or space or whatever is designated in the pattern).

Stitch Counts

Sometimes the turning chain that is worked at the end (or beginning) of a row or a round will be referred to as 1 stitch and it is then counted in the stitch count. In those cases, you will work into the next stitch, thus skipping the first stitch of the row or round. When the turning chain is not counted as a stitch, work into the first actual stitch.

Stitches Described

Sometimes the stitches are described as sc, dc, tr, ch-2 loop, 2-dc group, etc. and sometimes—such as in a mesh pattern of sc, ch 1—each sc and each ch 1 will be referred to as a st.

Back Loop

Along the top of each crochet stitch or chain there are two loops. The loop furthest away from you is the "back loop."

Front Loop

Along the top of each crochet stitch or chain there are two loops. The loop closest to you is the "front loop."

Joining New Colors

When joining new colors in crochet, whether at the beginning of a row or while working across, always work the stitch in the old color to the last 2 loops, then draw the new color through the 2 loops and continue with the new color.

Working Over Ends

Crochet has a unique flat top along each row that is perfect for laying the old color across and working over the ends for several stitches. This will alleviate the need to cut and weave in ends later.

Form a Ring

When a pattern is worked in the round, as in a square or medallion, the beginning chains are usually closed into a ring by working a slip stitch into the first chain. Then on the first round, stitches are usually worked into the ring and less often into each chain.

BLOCKING

Blocking crochet is usually not necessary. However, in those cases when you do need to smooth out the fabric, choose a blocking method consistent with information on the yarn care label and, when in doubt, test your gauge swatch. Note that some yarns, such as chenilles and ribbons, do not benefit from blocking.

Wet Block Method

Using rustproof pins, pin scarf to measurements on a flat surface and lightly dampen using a spray bottle. Allow to dry before removing pins.

Steam Block Method

Pin scarf to measurements with wrong side of the fabric facing up. Steam lightly, holding the iron 2"/5cm above the work. Do not press the iron directly onto the piece, as it will flatten the stitches.

Refer to the yarn label for the recommended cleaning method. Many of the scarves in the book can be washed by hand (or in the machine on a gentle or wool cycle) in lukewarm water with a mild detergent. Do not agitate, and don't soak for more than 10 minutes. Rinse gently with tepid water, then fold in a towel and gently press the water out. Lay flat to dry, away from excessive heat and light.

FRINGE

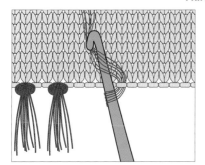

SIMPLE FRINGE: Cut yarn twice desired length plus extra for knotting. On wrong side, insert hook from front to back through piece and over folded yarn. Pull yarn through. Draw ends through and tighten. Trim yarn.

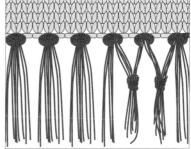

KNOTTED FRINGE: After working a simple fringe (it should be longer to allow for extra knotting), take one half of the strands from each fringe and knot them with half the strands from the neighboring fringe.

CHAIN

I *Pass the yarn over the hook and catch it with the hook.*

2 *Draw the yarn through the loop on the hook.*

3 *Repeat steps 1 and 2 to make a chain.*

SINGLE CROCHET

I *Insert the hook through top two loops of a stitch. Pass the yarn over the hook and draw up a loop—two loops on hook.*

2 *Pass the yarn over the hook and draw through both loops on hook.*

3 *Continue in the same way, inserting the hook into each stitch.*

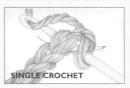

HALF-DOUBLE CROCHET

I *Pass the yarn over the hook. Insert the hook through the top two loops of a stitch.*

2 *Pass the yarn over the hook and draw up a loop—three loops on hook. Pass the yarn over the hook.*

3 *Draw through all three loops on hook.*

DOUBLE CROCHET

I *Pass the yarn over the hook. Insert the hook through the top two loops of a stitch.*

2 *Pass the yarn over the hook and draw up a loop—three loops on hook.*

3 *Pass the yarn over the hook and draw it through the first two loops on the hook, pass the yarn over the hook and draw through the remaining two loops. Continue in the same way, inserting the hook into each stitch.*

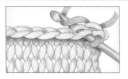

SLIP STITCH

Insert the crochet hook into a stitch, catch the yarn and pull up a loop. Draw the loop through the loop on the hook.

CROCHET TERMS AND ABBREVIATIONS

approx approximately

beg begin(ning)

CC contrast color

ch chain(s)

cm centimeter(s)

cont continue(ing)

dc double crochet (UK: tr-treble)

dec decrease(ing)–Reduce the stitches in a row (work stitches together or skip the stitches).

foll follow(s)(ing)

g gram(s)

hdc half double crochet (UK: htr-half treble)

inc increase(ing)–Add stitches in a row (work extra stitches into a stitch or between the stitches).

LH left-hand

lp(s) loop(s)

m meter(s)

MC main color

mm millimeter(s)

oz ounce(s)

pat(s) pattern

pm place markers–Place or attach a loop of contrast yarn or purchased stitch marker as indicated.

rem remain(s)(ing)

rep repeat

rnd(s) round(s)

RH right-hand

RS right side(s)

sc single crochet (UK: dc-double crochet)

sk skip

sl st slip stitch (UK: single crochet)

sp(s) space(s)

st(s) stitch(es)

t-ch turning chain

tog together

tr treble (UK: tr tr-triple treble)

WS wrong side(s)

work even Continue in pattern without increasing or decreasing. (UK: work straight)

yd yard(s)

yo yarn over–Wrap the yarn around the hook (UK: yrh)

* = Repeat directions following * as many times as indicated.

[ ] = Repeat directions inside brackets as many times as indicated.

Fringe festival

Created by Tanis Gray, this playful silk scarf adds a bright, festive feel to the dreariest winter day. Generous fringes enhance the pattern's whimsical style.

KNITTED MEASUREMENTS
■ Approx 4½"/11.5cm wide x 56"/142cm long (excluding fringe)

MATERIALS
■ 2 2oz/57g skeins (each approx 220yd/201m) of Fiesta Yarns *La Luz Multi* (silk) in wild oak ▨
■ Size G/6 (4mm) crochet hook *or size to obtain gauge*

GAUGE
6 cluster sts and 8 rows to 4½"/11.5cm over cluster pat st using size G/6 (4mm) crochet hook.
Take time to check gauge.

SCARF
Ch 28.

Row 1 Work 3 dc in 4th ch from hook, *sk next 3 ch, sc in next ch, ch 3, work 3 dc in same ch as sc; rep from *, end sk next 3 ch, sc in last ch—6 cluster sts. Ch 3, turn.
Row 2 Work 3 dc in first sc, *sc in next ch-3 sp, ch 3, work 3 dc in same ch-3 sp as sc; rep from *, end sc in ch-3 t-ch of row below. Ch 3, turn. Rep row 2 for cluster pat st until piece measures 56"/142cm from beg. Fasten off.

FINISHING
Block scarf lightly to measurements.

FRINGE
Cut 13"/33cm strands of yarn. Using 10 strands for each fringe, attach 5 fringes evenly spaced across each end of scarf. Trim ends evenly.

Whether you're lounging around or out on the town, you'll feel right at home in this classic design by Marty Miller.

KNITTED MEASUREMENTS
■ Approx 7"/17.5cm wide x 63"/160cm long (excluding fringe)

MATERIALS
■ 7 1¾oz/50g balls (each approx 92yds/84m) of Tahki Yarns/Tahki •Stacy Charles, Inc. *New Tweed* (wool/silk/viscose) in #46 ruby (4)
■ Size I/9 (5.5mm) crochet hook *or size to obtain gauge*

GAUGE
15 sts and 10 rows to 4"/10cm over basketweave pat using size I/9 (5.5mm) crochet hook.
Take time to check gauge.

STITCH GLOSSARY
Front post double crochet (FPdc)
Yo, insert hook from front to back to front around post of st of row below, yo and draw up a lp, [yo and draw through 2 lps] twice.

Back post double crochet (BPdc)
Yo, insert hook from back to front to back around post of st of row below, yo and draw up a lp, [yo and draw through 2 lps] twice.

SCARF
Ch 29.

Foundation row (WS) Dc in 4th ch from hook and in each ch across—26 dc. Ch 2, turn.

Row 1 Hdc in first st, *FPdc around next 4 sts, BPdc around next 4 sts; rep from * twice more, end hdc in last st. Ch 2, turn.

Rows 2 and 3 Rep row 1.

Rows 4–7 Hdc in first st, *BPdc around next 4 sts, FPdc around next 4 sts; rep from * twice more, end hdc in last st. Ch 2, turn.

Rows 8–11 Rep row 1. Rep rows 4–11 18 times more, then rows 4–7 once; piece should measure approx 63"/160cm from beg. Fasten off.

FINISHING
Block scarf lightly to measurements.

FRINGE
Cut 12"/30.5cm strands of yarn. Using 4 strands for each fringe, attach 7 fringes evenly spaced across each end of scarf. Trim ends evenly.

■■■ ■■ ■■ ■■

This charming scarf by Candi Jensen is enhanced by a delicate flower-petal motif, playfully extended on both ends.

KNITTED MEASUREMENTS
■ Approx 3"/7.5cm wide x 44"/111.5cm long (excluding fringe)

MATERIALS
■ 1 1¾oz/50g ball (each approx 124yd/113m) of Rowan Yarn/ Westminster Fibers, Inc. *Wool Cotton* (wool/cotton) each in #900 antique (MC), #901 citron (A) and #951 tender (B) ③
■ Size G/6 (4mm) crochet hook *or size to obtain gauge*

GAUGE
19 sts to 5"/12.5cm and 7 rows to 3"/7.5cm over hdc using size G/6 (4mm) crochet hook.
Take time to check gauge.

Notes
1 Scarf is made lengthways.
2 When changing colors, draw new color through last 2 lps on hook.

SCARF
With MC, ch 169.
Foundation row (WS) Hdc in 3rd ch from hook and in each ch across—167 sts. Ch 2, turn.

Row 1 Hdc in first st, *ch 1, sk next st, hdc in next st; rep from * across. Ch 2, turn.
Row 2 Hdc in each st and ch-1 sp across. Ch 2, turn. Rep rows 1 and 2 twice more. Fasten off.

FINISHING
Block scarf lightly to measurements.

Fringe and stripes
Each stripe is worked in chain st. Take care to maintain st gauge as you work. Position scarf so RS is facing and side edge (last row of scarf) is at top. For first fringe and stripe, with A, ch 30 for fringe. Insert hook into first ch-1 sp of row 1.
Row 1 Bring free end of yarn to WS of work, yo, draw through a lp and through lp on hook, *insert hook into next ch-1 sp, yo, draw through a lp and through lp on hook; rep from * across. Ch 20 for fringe. Fasten off. For 2nd fringe and stripe, with A, ch 14 for fringe. Insert hook into first ch-1 sp of row 3. Rep row 1 as for first fringe and stripe. Ch 28 for fringe. Fasten off. For 3rd fringe and stripe, with A, ch 24 for fringe. Insert hook into first ch-1 sp of row 5. Rep row 1 as for first fringe and stripe. Ch 13 for fringe. Fasten off.

Side fringe and edging
Row 1 (RS) With A, ch 30 for fringe, sc in first st of last row of scarf, then sc each st across, ch 35 for fringe. Fasten off. Turn

scarf so bottom edge is at top. **Row 1 (RS)** With A, ch 30 for fringe, sc between first and 2nd sts of foundation row, then sc between each st across, ch 35 for fringe. Fasten off.

Large rosebuds

Join B with a sl st in end of first fringe at right. **Rnd 1** Ch 7, work 4 dc in 3rd ch from hook, work 4 dc in next 3 ch, sc in last ch, changing to A. **Rnd 2** Ch 3, work 10 dc in same ch as sc, join rnd with a sl st in 3rd ch of beg ch-3. Fasten off. Make a large rosebud in every other fringe at each end of scarf.

Small rosebuds

Join B with a sl st in end of 2nd fringe at right. **Rnd 1** Ch 6, work 4 dc in 3rd ch from hook, work 4 dc in next 2 ch, sc in last ch, changing to A. **Rnd 2** Ch 3, work 8 dc in same ch as sc, join rnd with a sl st in 3rd ch of beg ch-3. Fasten off. Make a small rosebud in each rem fringe at each end of scarf.

Flowers (make 8 pieces)

With B, ch 4. Join ch with a sl st forming a ring. **Rnd 1** [Ch 4, sc in ring] 5 times. Fasten off. Arrange flowers as shown, then sew in place.

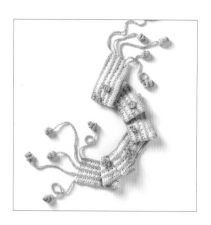

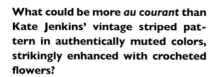

What could be more *au courant* than Kate Jenkins' vintage striped pattern in authentically muted colors, strikingly enhanced with crocheted flowers?

KNITTED MEASUREMENTS

■ Approx 6½"/16.5cm wide x 65"/165cm long (excluding flowers and leaves)

MATERIALS

■ 1 1¾oz/50g ball (each approx 95yd/87m) of Jaeger/Westminster Fibers, Inc. *Extra Fine Merino Aran* (wool) each in #546 wineberry (A), #540 blue star (B), #552 dahlia (C), #550 juniper (D), #538 garlic (E), #555 gold (F) and #551 pandora (G) **(4)**

■ Size J/10 (6mm) crochet hook *or size to obtain gauge*

GAUGE

17 sts to 5"/12.5cm and 9 rows to 4"/10cm over dc using size J/10 (6mm) crochet hook.

Take time to check gauge.

Notes

1 Scarf is worked lengthways.

2 When changing colors, draw new color through last 2 lps on hook, then ch and turn.

STITCH GLOSSARY

tr5tog [Yo twice, insert hook into next st and draw up lp, (yo, draw through 2 lps on hook) twice] 5 times, yo and draw through all 6 lps on hook.

dc2tog [Yo, insert hook into next st and draw up lp, yo, draw through 2 lps on hook] twice, yo and draw through all 3 lps on hook.

dc3tog [Yo, insert hook into next st and draw up lp, yo, draw through 2 lps on hook] 3 times, yo and draw through all 4 lps on hook.

SCARF

With A, ch 223.

Row 1 Dc in 4th ch from hook and in ch across, changing to B—220 sts. Ch 3, turn.

Row 2 Dc in each st across, changing to C. Ch 3, turn.

Rep row 2 for pat st and work stripe pat as foll: 1 row each in C, D, E, F, G, A, B, C, D, E, F, G. Fasten off.

FLOWERS

(make 10 pieces)

Center

With A, ch 7. Join ch with a sl st forming a ring.

Rnd 1 (RS) Ch 3 (counts as 1 dc), work 4 dc in ring, [ch 2, work 5 dc in ring] 4 times, ch 2, join rnd with a sl st in 3rd ch of beg ch-3—5 ch-2 sps. Fasten off.

Petals

With RS facing, join G with a sl st in any ch-2 sp.

Rnd 2 [Ch 6, tr5tog, ch 6, sl st in next ch-sp] 5 times—5 petals. Fasten off. Make 1 more flower using A for center and G for petals. Make 2 more flowers each using E for center and A for petals, F for center and B for petals, B for center and G for petals, and F for center and A for petals.

(make 14 pieces)

With D, ch 3.

Row I Work 3 dc in 3rd ch from hook. Ch 2, turn.

Row 2 Work 2 dc in first st, dc in next st, work 2 dc in last st—5 dc. Ch 2, turn.

Row 3 Work 2 dc in first st, dc in next 3 sts, work 2 dc in last st—7 dc, Ch 2, turn.

Row 4 Dc in each st across. Ch 2, turn.

Row 5 Dc2tog, dc in next 3 sts, dc2tog—5 dc. Ch 2, turn.

Row 6 Dc2tog, dc in next st, dc2tog—3 dc. Ch 2, turn.

Row 7 Dc3tog. Fasten off. Make 7 more leaves using D and 6 more using F.

FINISHING

Block scarf lightly to measurements. Referring to photo, arrange 5 flowers and 7 leaves on each end of scarf. Sew pieces in place using yarn colors to match.

EASY SCARF

Aqua mesh

Chi Ling Moy evokes the calm of the ocean with this captivating, impossibly soft mohair accessory.

KNITTED MEASUREMENTS

■ Approx 7"/17.5cm wide x 56"/142cm long

MATERIALS

■ 1 3½oz/100g ball (each approx 440yd/402m) of Alchemy Yarns of Transformation *Promise* (kid mohair/nylon) in #34w turquoise pool ⑤

■ Size C/2 (2.75mm) crochet hook *or size to obtain gauge*

GAUGE

9 dc and ch-2 sps, and 9 rows to 4"/10cm over mesh pat st using size C/2 (2.75mm) crochet hook.

Take time to check gauge.

SCARF

Ch 53.

Row 1 Dc in 8th ch (counts as ch 2, sk 2 ch and 1 dc) from hook, *ch 2, sk next 2 ch, dc in next ch; rep from * to end—16 ch-2 sps. Turn.

Row 2 Ch 5 (counts as 1 dc and ch 2), sk first 2 ch, *dc in next dc, ch 2; rep from *, end sk last 2 ch, dc in 3rd ch of t-ch of row below. Turn. Rep row 2 for mesh pat st until piece measures 56"/142cm from beg. Fasten off.

FINISHING

Block scarf lightly to measurements.

Kathleen Stuart has designed a bold, striking pattern that works equally well on snowy slopes or in a four-star restaurant.

KNITTED MEASUREMENTS
■ Approx 7½"/19cm wide x 59"/150cm long

MATERIALS
■ 1 6oz/170g skein (each approx 330yd/ 302m) of Caron International *Simply Soft Solids* (acrylic) each in #9727 black (A) and #9702 off white (B) (④)
■ Size J/10 (6mm) crochet hook *or size to obtain gauge*

GAUGE
13 sts and 16 rows to 4"/10cm over pat st using size J/10 (6mm) crochet hook. *Take time to check gauge.*

Notes

1 When changing colors, draw new color through last 2 lps on hook.

2 Carry color not in use along side edge of work.

STITCH GLOSSARY
Long double crochet (Ldc) Yo, insert hook from front to back in st indicated, yo and draw up a long lp, [yo and draw through 2 lps on hook] twice.

SCARF
With A, ch 26.

Row 1 Sc in 2nd ch from hook and in each ch across, changing to B in last st—25 sts. Ch 1, turn.

Row 2 Sc in each st across. Ch 1, turn

Row 3 Rep row 2, changing to A in last st. Ch 1, turn.

Row 4 Sc in first st, Ldc in 3rd sc of 3 rows below, *sc in next st on working row, Ldc in 2nd st from previous Ldc 3 rows below, sc in next st on working row, Ldc in same st as previous Ldc, sc in next st on working row, Ldc in 2nd st from previous Ldc 3 rows below, sc in next st on working row, Ldc in 4th st from previous Ldc 3 rows below; rep from * once more, end sc in next st on working row, Ldc in 2nd st from previous Ldc 3 rows below, sc in next st on working row, Ldc in same st as previous Ldc, sc in next st on working row, Ldc in 2nd st from previous Ldc 3 rows below, sc in last st on working row. Ch 1, turn.

Row 5 Sc in each sc across, changing to B in last st. Ch 1, turn.

Row 6 Rep row 4.

Row 7 Rep row 5, changing to A in last st. Ch 1, turn. Rep rows 4 to 7 for pat st and stripe pat until piece measures 59"/150cm from beg, end with row 4. Fasten off.

FINISHING
Block scarf lightly to measurements.

Slinky snake

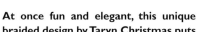

At once fun and elegant, this unique braided design by Taryn Christmas puts a beautiful twist on the traditional scarf.

KNITTED MEASUREMENTS
■ Approx 4"/10cm wide x 60"/152.5cm long (excluding fringe)

MATERIALS
■ 2 1¾oz/50g balls (each approx 95yd/ 87m) of Trendsetter Yarns *Pepita* (polyamid/acrylic) each in #982 purple medley(A), #187 chocolate almond (B) and #222 desert sunset (C)
■ Size L/11 (8mm) afghan hook *or size to obtain gauge*

GAUGE
6 sts to 1¾"/4.5cm and 16 rows to 4"/10cm over tunisian knit st using size L/11 (8mm) afghan hook.
Take time to check gauge.

Note
Each row of tunisian knit st is worked in two halves. The first half is worked from right to left and the second half is worked from left to right.

STRIP
(make 3 pieces)
With A, ch 6.
Row 1 (first half) Retaining all lps on hook, insert hook into 2nd ch from hook, yo and draw up a lp, *insert hook into next ch, yo and draw up a lp; rep from * across—6 lps on hook.
Row 1 (second half) Yo, draw through first lp on hook, *yo and draw through next 2 lps on hook; rep from * until 1 lp rem on hook.
Row 2 (first half) Retaining all lps on hook, sk first pair of vertical threads, *insert hook between next pair of vertical threads, yo and draw up a lp; rep from * across.
Row 2 (second half) Yo, draw through first lp on hook, *yo and draw through next 2 lps on hook; rep from * until 1 lp rem on hook. Rep row 2 for tunisian knit st until piece measures 70"/178cm from beg.
Last row Sk first pair of vertical threads, *insert hook between next pair of vertical threads, yo and draw up a lp, yo and draw through both lps on hook; rep from * across. Fasten off. Make 2 more strips using B and C.

FINISHING
Block strips lightly to measurements. Place strips side by side on work surface, with A at left, B in center and C at right. Sew side edges of strips tog for 3½"/9cm. Braid strips to within 3½"/9cm of ends. Sew edges of strips tog for 3½"/9cm to secure braiding.

FRINGE
Cut 14"/35.5cm strands of each color. Using one strand of color for each fringe, attach 13 fringes evenly spaced across each end of scarf. Trim ends evenly.

■■■■▭

Whether it's flying in the wind or wrapped snugly around you, this spirited piece by Veronica Manno will add flair to any ensemble.

KNITTED MEASUREMENTS
■ Approx 7"/17.5cm wide x 45"/114.5cm long (excluding fringe)

MATERIALS
■ 4 1¾oz/50g balls (each approx 120yd/110m) of GGH/Muench Yarns *Maxima* (wool) in #42 blue ⬛③
■ Size H/8 (5mm) afghan hook *or size to obtain gauge*

GAUGE
20 sts and 14 rows to 4"/10cm over tunisian (afghan) st using size H/8 (5mm) afghan hook.
Take time to check gauge.

Note

Each row of tunisian (afghan) st is worked in two halves. The first half is worked from right to left and the second half is worked from left to right.

SCARF

Ch 35.
Row 1 (first half) Retaining all lps on hook, insert hook into 2nd ch from hook, yo and draw up a lp, *insert hook into next ch, yo and draw up a lp; rep from * across—35 lps on hook.

Row 1 (second half) Yo, draw through first lp on hook, *yo and draw through next 2 lps on hook; rep from * until 1 lp rem on hook.

Row 2 (first half) Retaining all lps on hook, insert hook under 2nd vertical thread from side edge of the previous row, yo and draw up a lp, *insert hook under next vertical thread, yo and draw up a lp; rep from * across. Turn.

Row 2 (second half) Yo, draw through first lp on hook, *yo and draw through next 2 lps on hook; rep from * until 1 lp rem on hook. Rep row 2 for tunisian (afghan) st until piece measures 45"/114.5cm from beg.

Last row Insert hook under 2nd vertical thread from side edge of the previous row, yo and draw up a lp, yo and draw through both lps on hook, *insert hook under next vertical thread, yo and draw up a lp, yo and draw through both lps on hook; rep from * across. Fasten off.

FINISHING

Block scarf lightly to measurements.

FRINGE

Cut 15"/38cm strands of yarn. Using 3 strands for each fringe, attach 17 fringes evenly spaced across each end of scarf. Trim ends evenly.

Bead it

Stand out from the crowd with this eye-catching scarf by Kristen TenDyke, adorned with simple yet striking wooden beads.

KNITTED MEASUREMENTS

■ Approx 4½"/11.5cm wide x 61"/155cm long (excluding fringe)

MATERIALS

■ 2 1¾oz/50g hanks (each approx 123yd/113m) of Classic Elite Yarns *Lush* (angora/wool) in #4413 black 〔4〕

■ Size H/8 (5mm) crochet hook *or size to obtain gauge*

■ Two hundred and thirty (eight 15"/38cm strands) of 11 x 12mm brown wooden barrel beads

GAUGE

6 dc and ch-2 sps, and 9 rows to 4"/10cm over mesh pat st using size H/8 (5mm) crochet hook.
Take time to check gauge.

Note

Scarf is worked lengthways.

STITCH GLOSSARY

Place bead (PB) Slip bead onto hook, yo, loosely draw up a lp through bead and through lp on hook

SCARF

Ch 277 sts.

Row 1 (RS) Dc in 8th ch from hook, *ch 2, sk next 2 ch, dc in ch; rep from * to end—92 dc and 91 ch-2 sps. Turn.

Row 2 Ch 5 (counts as 1 dc and ch 2), sk first dc, dc in next dc, *PB, ch 1, dc in next dc, ch 2, dc in next dc; rep from *, ending last rep with dc in 3rd ch of t-ch. Turn.

Row 3 Ch 5 (counts as 1 dc and ch 2), sk first dc, dc into next dc, *ch 2, dc in next dc; rep from *, ending last rep with dc in 3rd ch of t-ch. Turn.

Row 4 Ch 3 (counts as 1 dc), PB, ch 1, dc in first dc, *ch 2, dc in next dc, PB, ch 1, dc in next dc; rep from *, ending last rep with dc in 3rd ch of t-ch. Turn.

Row 5 Rep row 3.

Rows 6–11 Rep rows 2–5 once more, then rows 2 and 3 once. Fasten off.

FRINGE

Cut 10"/25.5cm strands of yarn. Using 1 strand for each fringe, attach 22 fringes evenly spaced across each end of scarf. Trim ends evenly.

Slinky, sassy, and impossible to miss, this faux boa by Taryn Christmas blends a fearless, contemporary feel with a timeless design.

KNITTED MEASUREMENTS

■ Approx 3½"/9cm wide x 76"/193cm long

MATERIALS

■ 3 1¾oz/50g balls (each approx 120yd/110m) of Anny Blatt *Assouan* (cotton) in #511 rubis (A) ③

■ 5 balls each in #115 coquelicot (B) and #876 salsa (C)

■ Size G/6 (4mm) crochet hook *or size to obtain gauge*

GAUGE

22 sts to 4"/10cm and 3 rows to 2½"/6.5cm over ruffle pat using size G/6 (4mm) crochet hook.
Take time to check gauge.

STITCH GLOSSARY

Double treble crochet (dtr)

Yo 3 times, insert hook into st, yo and draw up a lp, [yo and draw through 2 lps on hook] 4 times.

SCARF

With A, crochet a 70"/178cm long ch.

Row 1 (RS) Dtr in 5th ch from hook, work 4 dtr in same ch, *work 5 dtr in next ch; rep from * across. Fasten off.

Row 2 With RS facing, join B with a sl st in first st, ch 3, work 2 tr in same st as joining, *work 3 tr in next st; rep from * across. Fasten off.

Row 3 With RS facing, join C with a sl st in first st, ch 1, hdc in same st as joining, *work 2 hdc in next st; rep from * across. Fasten off.

Indulge your inner child with this delightfully playful penguin design by Kathleen Stuart, complete with beaded eyes and tiny little feet!

■ Approx 5"/12.5cm wide x 43"/109cm long

MATERIALS

■ 2 3oz/85g skeins (each approx 158yd/144m) of Lion Brand Yarns *Lion Wool* (wool) each in #153 ebony (A) and #99 winter white (B) **(4)**

■ 1 skein in #133 pumpkin (C)

■ Size J/10 (6mm) crochet hook *or size to obtain gauge*

■ One pair of 12mm brown sew-on animal eyes

■ Small amount of polyester fiberfill

■ Small safety pin

GAUGE

18 sts to 5"/12.5cm and 17 rows to 4"/10cm over sc using size J/10 (6mm) crochet hook.

Take time to check gauge.

Note

When changing colors, draw new color through 2 lps on hook to complete sc.

STITCH GLOSSARY

sc2tog [Insert hook into next st and draw up a lp] twice, yo and draw through all 3 lps on hook.

SCARF

Beak

With C, ch 2.

Rnd 1 Work 6 sc in 2nd ch from hook. Mark last st made with the safety pin. You will be working in a spiral marking the last st made with the safety pin to indicate end of rnd.

Rnd 2 [Sc in next st, work 2 sc in next st] 3 times—9 sts.

Rnd 3 Sc in each st around.

Rnd 4 [Sc in next 2 sts, work 2 sc in next st] 3 times—12 sts.

Rnds 5 Sc in each st around, changing to A in last st.

Head

Rnd 6 Working in back lps only, [sc in next st, work 2 sc in next st] 6 times—18 sts.

Rnd 7 [Sc in next 2 sts, work 2 sc in next st] 6 times—24 sts.

Rnd 8 [Sc in next 3 sts, 2 sc in next st] 6 times—30 sts.

Rnds 9–12 Sc in each st around.

Rnd 13 [Sc in next 3 sts, sc2tog] 6 times—24 sts.

Rnd 14 [Sc in next 2 sts, sc2tog] 6 times—18 sts.

Rnd 15 Working in back lps only [sc in next st, sc2tog] 6 times—12 sts.

Rnd 16 [Sc2tog] 6 times—6 sts. Remove safety pin. Fasten off leaving a long tail. Stuff head and beak lightly. Thread tail into tapestry needle and weave through sts. Pull tight to gather, fasten off securely.

Body

You will be working in the free front lps of rnd 14.

Rnd 17 Join A with a sl st in front lp of the 10th st, ch 4. Fasten off. Join A with a sl st in front lp of the first st, ch 5, turn. Sc in 2nd ch from hook, sc in next 3 ch, sc in front lps of the next 9 sts, sc in first 3 ch of attached ch-4, work 2 sc in last ch changing to B, sc in same ch as last 2 sc. Working in bottom lps of ch, sc in next 3 bottom lps, sc in same st as sl st on rnd 14, sc in free lps of next 8 sts, working in bottom lps of next ch, sc in next 3 bottom lps, then work 2 sc in last bottom lp, join rnd with a sl st in first sc—36 sts (18 sts in A and 18 sts in B). Ch 1, turn.

Rnd 18 Sc in first 18 sts changing to A, sc in last 18 sts, join rnd with a sl st in first sc. Ch 1, turn.

Rnd 19 Sc in first 18 sts changing to B, sc in last 18 sts, join rnd with a sl st in first sc.

Rnds 20–159 Rep rnds 18 and 19.

Rnd 160 Rep rnd 18. Ch 1, turn.

Tail

Rnd 161 [Sc2tog] 9 times changing to B, [sc2tog] 9 times, join rnd with a sl st in first sc—18 sts. Ch 1, turn.

Rnd 162 Sc in first 9 sts changing to A, sc in last 9 sts, join rnd with a sl st in first sc. Ch 1, turn.

Rnd 163 [Sc in next 2 sts, work 2 sc in next st] 3 times changing to B, [sc in next 2 sts, work 2 sc in next st] 3 times, join rnd with a sl st in first sc—24 sts. Ch 1, turn.

Rnd 164 Sc in first 12 sts changing to A, sc in last 12 sts, join rnd with a sl st in first sc. Ch 1, turn.

Rnd 165 [Sc in next 3 sts, work 2 sc in next st] 3 times changing to B, [sc in next 3 sts, work 2 sc in next st] 3 times, join rnd with a sl st in first sc—30 sts. Ch 1, turn.

Rnd 166 Sc in first 15 sts changing to A, sc in last 15 sts, join rnd with a sl st in first sc. Ch 1, turn.

Rnd 167 [Sc in next 4 sts, work 2 sc in next st] 3 times changing to B, [sc in next 4 sts, work 2 sc in next st] 3 times, join rnd with a sl st in first sc—36 sts. Ch 1, turn.

Rnd 168 Sc in first 18 sts changing to A, sc in last 18 sts, join rnd with a sl st in first sc. Ch 1, turn.

Joining

Bring A and B edges tog matching sts. Working through both thicknesses, sc in 18 sts across. Fasten off.

FEET

(make 2 pieces)

Beg at top edge, with C, ch 5.

Row 1 Sc in 2nd ch from hook and in each ch across—4 sts. Ch 1, turn.

Row 2 Sc in first st, ch 2, sc in 2nd ch from hook, sc in next st of row 1, ch 3, sc in 2nd ch from hook and in next ch, sc in next st of row 1, ch 2, sc in 2nd ch from hook, sc in last st of row 1. Fasten off leaving a long tail for sewing.

FINISHING

Block scarf lightly to measurements. Sew on eyes. On B side, position feet so top edges are one row below beg of tail shaping. Sew top edges of feet in place.

Rich, chunky cables and a medium-length fringe come together in this classic neck warmer by Karen J. Hay.

KNITTED MEASUREMENTS

■ Approx 4½"/11.5cm wide x 56"/142cm long (excluding fringe)

MATERIALS

■ 4 1¾oz/50g balls (each approx 109yd/100m) of Dale of Norway *Heilo* (wool) in #5813 light blue (3)

■ Size G/6 (4.5mm) crochet hook *or size to obtain gauge*

GAUGE

19 sts and 8 rows to 4"/10cm over cable pat using size G/6 (4mm) crochet hook. *Take time to check gauge.*

STITCH GLOSSARY

Front post treble crochet (FPtr) Yo twice, insert hook from front to back to front around post of specified st of row below, yo and draw up a lp, [yo and draw through 2 lps] three times.

Back post treble crochet (BPtr) Yo twice, insert hook from back to front to back around post (vertical bar) of specified st of row below, yo and draw up a lp, [yo and draw through 2 lps] three times.

SCARF

Ch 25.

Row 1 (WS) Dc in 4th ch from hook and in each ch across—22 dc. Ch 3, turn.

Row 2 Dc in first st, sk next 2 sts, FPtr around next 2 sts, FPtr around first sk st, then around 2nd sk st, FPtr around next 2 sts, *dc in next st, sk next 2 sts, FPtr around next 2 sts, FPtr around first sk st, then around 2nd sk st, FPtr around next 2 sts; rep from * once more, end dc in last st—3 6-st cables made. Ch 3, turn.

Row 3 Dc in first st, sk first 2 sts, BPtr around next 2 sts, BPtr around 2nd sk st, then 2d sk st, BPtr around next 2 sts, *dc in next dc, sk next 2 sts, BPtr around next 2 sts, BPtr in 2 skipped tr, BPtr in next 2 tr, rep from * once more, dc in last dc. Ch 3, turn. Rep rows 2 and 3 for cable pat until piece measures approx 56"/142cm from beg. Ch 3, turn.

Last row Dc in each st across. Fasten off.

FINISHING

Block scarf lightly to measurements.

FRINGE

Cut 10"/25.5cm strands of yarn. Using 10 strands for each fringe, attach 7 fringe evenly spaced across each end of scarf. Trim ends evenly.

■■■□

Delicate but durable, this graceful design by Kristen TenDyke evokes the charm of days past.

KNITTED MEASUREMENTS
■ Approx 9½"/24cm wide x 65"/165cm long

MATERIALS
■ 4 1¾oz/50g hanks (each approx 93yd/85m) of Classic Elite Yarns *Flash* (cotton) in #6188 coral rose (**4**)
■ Size H/8 (5mm) crochet hook *or size to obtain gauge*

GAUGE
One motif is 5¼"/13.5cm across using size H/8 (5mm) crochet hook.
Take time to check gauge.

MOTIF A

Ch 4 (counts as 1 dc and 1 ch).

Rnd I (WS) Work 11 dc in 4th ch from hook, join rnd with a sl st in 3rd ch of beg ch-4—12 dc. Turn.

Rnd 2 (RS) Ch 7 (counts as 1 dc and ch 4), *sk next st, dc in next st, ch 4; rep from * around, join rnd with a sl st in 3rd ch of beg ch-6—6 ch-4 sps.

Rnd 3 Sl st in first ch-sp, ch 3 (counts as 1 dc), work 4 dc in same ch-sp, *ch 4, work 5 dc into next ch-sp; rep from * 4 times more, to join rnd, ch 1, dc in 3rd ch of beg ch-3 (counts as 1 ch-4 sp)—6 ch-4 sps.

Rnd 4 Ch 3 (counts as 1 dc), work 2 dc in ch-sp created by dc, *ch 4, work (3 dc, ch 3, 3 dc) in next ch-sp; rep from * 4 times more, end ch 4, work 3 dc in beg ch-sp, to join rnd, dc in 3rd ch of beg ch-3 (counts as 1 ch-3 sp)—6 ch-3 sps and 6 ch-4 sps.

Rnd 5 *Ch 5, sl st in ch-4 sp, ch 5, sl st in next ch-3 sp; rep from * around, end ch 5, join rnd with a sl st in joining dc of rnd 4—12 ch-5 sps. Fasten off.

MOTIF B

Work as for motif A through rnd 4.

Joining

Rnd 5 Ch 5, sl st in first ch-4 sp, ch 2, sl st in any ch-5 sp of motif A, ch 2, sl st into next ch-3 sp of motif B, ch 2, sl st in next ch-5 of motif A, ch 2, sl st in next ch-4 sp of motif B, cont to work motif B as foll: *ch 5, sl st in next ch-3 sp, ch 5, sl st in next ch-4 sp; rep from * around, end ch 5, join rnd with a sl st in joining dc of rnd 4—12 ch-5 sps. Fasten off.

MOTIF C

Work as for motif A through rnd 4.

Joining

Rnd 5 Ch 5, sl st in first ch-4 sp, ch 2, sl st in ch-5 sp of motif B opposite joining of motifs A and B, ch 2, sl st in next ch-3 sp of motif C, ch 2, sl st in next ch-5 sp of motif B, ch 2, sl st in next ch-4 sp of motif C, cont to work motif C as foll: *ch 5, sl st in next ch-3 sp, ch 5, sl st in next ch-4 sp; rep from * around, end ch 5, join rnd with a sl st in joining dc of rnd 4—12 ch-5 sps. Fasten off. Referring to assembly diagram, cont to join 8 more motifs forming a strip of 11 motifs.

MOTIF D

Work as for motif A through rnd 4.

Joining

Rnd 5 Ch 5, sl st in first ch-4 sp, ch 2, sk ch-5 sp before joining of motifs A and B, sl st in next ch-5 sp of motif A, ch 2, sl st in next ch-3 sp of motif D, ch 2, sl st in next ch-5 sp of motif A, ch 2, sl st in next ch-4 sp of motif D, ch 2, sl st in next ch-5 sp of motif B, ch 2, sl st in next ch-3 sp of motif D, ch 2, sl st in next ch-5 sp of motif B, ch 2, sl st in next ch-4 sp of motif D, cont to work motif D as foll: *ch 5, sl st in next ch-3 sp, ch 5, sl st in next ch-4 sp; rep from * around, end ch 5, join rnd with a sl st in joining dc of rnd 4—12 ch-5 sps. Fasten off.

MOTIF E

Work as for motif A through rnd 4.

Joining

Rnd 5 Ch 5, sl st in first ch-4 sp, ch 2, sk ch-5 sp before joining of motifs C and D, sl st in next ch-5 sp of motif D, ch 2, sl st in next ch-3 sp of motif E, ch 2, sl st in next ch-5 sp of motif D, ch 2, sl st in next ch-4 sp of motif E, ch 2, sl st in next ch-5 sp of motif B, ch 2, sl st in next ch-3 sp of motif E, ch 2, sl st in next ch-5 sp of motif E, ch 2, sl st in next ch-4 sp of motif E, ch 2, sl st in next ch-5 sp of motif C, ch 2, sl st in next ch-3 sp of motif E, ch 2, sl st in next ch-5 sp of motif C, ch 2, sl st in next ch-4 sp of motif E, cont to work motif E as foll: *ch 5, sl st in next ch-3 sp, ch 5, sl st in next ch-4 sp; rep from * around, end ch 5, join rnd with a sl st in joining dc of rnd 4—12 ch-5 sps. Fasten off. Referring to assembly diagram, cont to join 8 more motifs to first strip of 11 motifs.

MOTIF F

Work as for motif A through rnd 4.

Joining

Rnd 5 Work as for motif E, joining motif to last motif C and motif E only. Fasten off. Piece should measure approx 65"/ 165cm from beg.

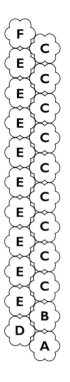

FINISHING

Block scarf lightly to measurements.

All wired up

Sasha Kagan's electrifying design will have you amped up with its fun pom-poms and internal "circuitry."

KNITTED MEASUREMENTS
■ Approx 7"/17.5cm wide x 42"/106.5cm long (excluding fringe)

MATERIALS
■ 2 1¾oz/50g balls (each approx 151yd/140m) of Rowan Yarn/ Westminster Fibers, Inc. *Kid Classic* (lambswool/kid mohair/nylon) in #835 royal (MC) ◼

■ 1 .87oz/25g ball (each approx 229yd/ 210m) of Rowan Yarn/ Westminster Fibers, Inc. *Kidsilk Haze* (kid mohair/ silk) each in #577 elegance (A), #595 liqueur (B) and #578 swish (C) ◼

■ Size G/6 (4mm) crochet hook *or size to obtain gauge*

GAUGE
19 sts to 5"/12.5cm and 11 rows to 4"/10cm over dc pat st using size G/6 (4mm) crochet hook.
Take time to check gauge.

SCARF
With MC, ch 165 loosely.
Row I (WS) Dc in 4th ch from hook and in each ch across—162 sts. Ch 3, turn.

Row 2 Working through back lps only, dc in each st across. Ch 3, turn.
Row 3 Working through front lps only. dc in each st across. Ch 3, turn. Rep rows 2 and 3 7 times more, then rep row 2 once— 18 rows and 17 horizontal ridges of free lps. Fasten off.

FINISHING
Block scarf lightly to measurements.
Top edging
With RS facing, join MC with a sl st in first st of row 18, ch 3, sl st in same st as joining, sl in next 3 sts, *ch 3, sl st in same st as last st, sl st in next 3 sts; rep from * across. Fasten off.
Bottom edging
With RS facing, join MC with a sl st in first bottom lp of foundation ch, ch 3, sl st in same lp as joining, sl in next 3 lps, *ch 3, sl st in same lp as last st, sl st in next 3 lps; rep from * across. Fasten off.
Fringe and squiggle embellishments
For first fringe/squiggle, join MC with a sl st in right side edge of center horizontal ridge of free lps; ch 20 and fasten off. Rep on left side edge. Join C with a sl st in first ch at right edge. **Row I** Ch 1, work 2 sc in same ch as joining, [work 2 sc in next ch] 19 times. Fold scarf along ridge of free lps, *work 2 sc in next free lp; rep from * to ch at left edge, [work 2 sc in next ch] 20

times. Ch 1, turn. **Row 2** Work 2 sc in each st across. Fasten off.

For second fringe/squiggle, skip 2 horizontal ridges up from first fringe/squiggle and join MC with a sl st in right side edge of next horizontal ridge; ch 20 and fasten off. Rep on left side edge. Cont to work as for first fringe/squiggle using B. For third fringe/squiggle, skip 2 horizontal ridges down from second fringe/squiggle and cont to work as for second fringe/squiggle using A.

For fourth fringe/squiggle, skip 2 horizontal ridges up from second fringe/squiggle and join MC with a sl st in right side edge of next horizontal ridge; ch 20 and fasten off. Rep on left side edge. Cont to work as for first fringe/squiggle using B. For fifth fringe/squiggle, skip 2 horizontal ridges down from third fringe/squiggle and cont to work as for fourth fringe/squiggle using C.

(make 10 pieces)

With B, make 2 pompoms 1½"/4cm in diameter. Sew one to each end of first fringe. Make 4 pompoms using C and sew one to each end of second and third fringes. Make 4 pompoms using A and sew one to each end of fourth and fifth fringes.

Evoking the green countryside, Gwen Blakley Kinsler puts a contemporary spin on a traditional Americana design.

■ Approx 5½"/14cm x 61"/155cm

■ 2 3½oz/100g balls (each approx 250yd/229m) of South West Trading Company *Bamboo* (bamboo) in #521 turquoise green (A) (**4**)

■ 1 1¾oz/50g ball (approx 98yd/89m) of South West Trading Company *Amerah* (silk) in #274 earth (B) (**4**)

■ 1 3½ oz/100g ball (approx 110yd/ 100m) of South West Trading Company *Twizé* (bamboo) in #329 twey (C) (**4**)

■ 1 1¾oz/50g ball (approx 80yd/73m) of South West Trading Company *Fur Real* (rayon/nylon/acrylic) each in flamingo (D) and peacock (E) (**4**)

■ Size I/9 and J/10 (5.5 and 6mm) crochet hooks *or sizes to obtain gauges*

18 st and 24 rows to 5"/12.5cm over moss st using smaller crochet hook. One motif is 3½"/9cm x 4"/10cm using larger crochet hook.
Take time to check gauge.

Note

When changing colors, draw new color through last 2 lps on hook to complete the st.

5-dc popcorn (PC) Work 5 dc in one st. Drop lp from hook. Insert hook into first dc, then place lp back on hook. Draw lp through st, then ch 1 to secure popcorn.

Back loop only (BLO) Insert hook in back lp of specified st to create a ridge on front of work.

Front loop only (FLO) Insert hook in front lp of specified st to create a ridge on front of work.

Chain a multiple of 2 ch plus 1.
Row 1 (WS) Sc in 2nd ch from hook, dc in next ch, *sc in next ch, dc in next ch; rep from * across. Ch 1, turn.
Row 2 *Sc in next dc, dc in next sc, rep from * across. Ch 1, turn.
Rep row 2 for moss st.

(make 2 pieces)
With larger hook and A, ch 4.
Rnd 1 (RS) Work 5 dc in 3rd ch from hook, work 3 PC in 4th ch from hook, dc in side edge of beg ch, hdc in next 2 sts, working BLO, work 2 dc in next st changing to B.

Rnd 2 Working BLO, work (dc, hdc) in next st, hdc in next 2 sts, work (sc, hdc) in next st, [work 2 dc in next st] twice, work (hdc, sc) in next st changing to C. Ch 1, turn.

Rnd 3 (WS) Sl st in first st, sc in next 2 sts, work (sc, hdc) in next st, hdc in next st, work (hdc, dc) in next st, dc in next 2 sts, work (dc, hdc) in next 2 sts, work 2 hdc in next st, sc in next st, sl st in next st changing to D.

Rnd 4 Sc in first 3 sts, working BLO, sc in next 3 sts, hdc in next st, work (hdc, dc, hdc) in next st, sc in next 3 sts, sl st in next st, sc in next 3 sts, hdc in next st, work 2 hdc in next st, sc in next st, sl st in next 2 sts changing to A.

Rnd 5 Working FLO, work (sc, hdc) in first st, work (hdc, dc) in next st, [work 2 dc in next st] twice, hdc in next st, sc in next 6 sts changing to E. Ch 1, turn.

Rnd 6 (RS) Working BLO, sl st in first 2 sts, sc in next 4 sts, hdc in next st, work (hdc, dc) in next st, dc in next 2 sts, work (dc,hdc) in next st, hdc in next 2 sts, sc in next 3 sts changing to B, sc in next 3 sts, work (hdc, sc) in next st, sc in next 11 sts,

work (hdc, dc, dc) in next st, sl st in next st changing to E. Ch 1, turn.

Rnd 7 (WS) Sk first st, working BLO, sl st in next st, work 2 sc in next st, sc in next 2 sts, hdc in next 3 sts, sc in next 3 sts, work 2 hdc in next st, hdc in next 2 sts, work 2 sc in next st, sc in next 2 sts, sl st in next st. Fasten off.

MOTIF II

(make 1 piece)

With larger hook and A, ch 4. Cont to work as for motif I changing colors as foll:

Rnd 1 Change to E at end of rnd.

Rnd 2 Change to D at end of rnd.

Rnd 3 Change to C at end of rnd.

Rnd 4 Change to A at end of rnd.

Rnd 5 Change to B at end of rnd.

Rnd 6 Change to E in middle of rnd, then to B at end of rnd.

Rnd 7 Work as for motif I. Fasten off.

SCARF

With smaller hook and A, ch 19. Work row 1 of moss st—18 sts. Work row 2 seven times. Ch 1, turn.

Insert first motif

Row 9 (WS) [Sc in next dc, dc in next sc]

twice, with WS of motif I facing, join next 9 sts of motif (the edge that's opposite the pointed end) to scarf by working through both lps of each scarf and motif st with a sl st, working scarf sts only, [dc in next sc, sc in next dc] twice, dc in last sc—18 sts. Ch 1, turn.

Row 10 (RS) Working on RH side of motif only, work in moss st across first 5 sts of scarf, sl st to edge of motif, sl st up to next st on motif. Turn.

Row 11 Work in moss st across 5 sts of scarf. Ch 1, turn.

Rows 12–23 Cont working in moss st and joining edge of motif with sl sts. (**Note** The amount of scarf sts will vary from row to row to accommodate the shape of the motif. Be careful to keep scarf edge straight by not adding or subtracting too many sts.) Fasten off. With RS facing, join A to other side of motif with a sl st, then work in moss st across rem scarf sts. Working on LH side of motif only, work as for RH side.

Row 24 (RS) Work 18 moss sts across. Ch 1, turn. Work even until piece measures 8½"/21.5cm from beg, end with a RS row.

Insert second motif

Insert motif II as for first motif, placing it at a different angle to create visual interest. When insertion is completed, work even with A only until piece measures 50"/127cm from beg, end with a RS row.

Insert third motif

Insert motif III as for first motif, placing it at a different angle. When insertion is completed, work even with A only until piece measures 60"/152.5cm from beg, end with a WS row. Ch 1, turn.

Edging

Rnd 1 (RS) Making sure that work lies flat, sc evenly around entire edge working 3 sc in each corner, join rnd with a sl st in first sc.

Rnd 2 Ch 1, working from left to right, sc in each st around, join rnd with a sl st in first sc. Fasten off.

FINISHING

Block scarf lightly to measurements.

WAVE PATTERN SCARF

Sangria sensation

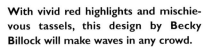

With vivid red highlights and mischievous tassels, this design by Becky Billock will make waves in any crowd.

KNITTED MEASUREMENTS

■ Approx 4½"/11.5cm wide x 65"/165cm long (excluding fringe)

MATERIALS

■ 3 1¾oz/50g skeins (each approx 89yd/82m) of Berroco *Touché* (rayon/cotton) in #7922 shiraz (A) ■

■ 2 1¾oz/50g balls (each approx 119yd/110m) of Berroco *Yoga* (nylon/polyester) in #6438 guru (B) ■

■ Size E/4 (3.5mm) crochet hook *or size to obtain gauge*

GAUGE

24 sts and 8 rows to 4"/10cm over base pat st using size E/4 (3.5mm) crochet hook.
Take time to check gauge.

Note

The scarf is made in two steps: first make a base scarf using A and working from the bottom up. Then work a ribbon chain embellishment over the base scarf using B and working from the top down.

BASE SCARF

With A, ch 34.

Row 1 Dc in 8th ch from hook, sc in next ch, dc in next ch, *ch 3, sk 3 next ch, dc in next ch, sc in next ch, dc in next ch; rep from * across. Ch 5, turn.

Row 2 Work (dc, sc, dc) in first ch-sp, *ch 3, work (dc, sc, dc) in next ch-sp; rep from * across. Ch 5, turn. Rep row 2 for base pat st until piece measures 65"/165cm from beg. Fasten off.

RIBBON CHAIN EMBELLISHMENT

Join B with a sl st in last sc of last row of base scarf. Turn.

Row 1 *Ch 6, sl st in next sc; rep from * across. Ch 7, turn base scarf so last row worked is at bottom and the ch-7 is at right. Fold last row of ch-6 lps to back of work.

Row 2 Keeping yarn in front, insert hook into first ch-sp of base scarf and under ch-7 t-ch, yo and draw up a lp, then through lp on hook making a sl st, *ch 5, insert hook into next ch-sp of base scarf and under next B ch-lp and make sl st; rep from * across. Ch 7, turn. Rep row 2 for ribbon chain embellishment st to next to last row of base scarf. Ch 7, turn. To end, insert hook into first ch-sp of base scarf and under ch-7 t-ch and make a sl st. Fasten off.

FINISHING
Block scarf lightly to measurements.

FRINGE
Cut 20"/51cm strands of B. Using 4 strands for each fringe, attach 10 fringes evenly spaced across each end of scarf, knotting fringe around both the base scarf ch-lps and the B ch-lps. Trim ends evenly.

■■■■▶

Playful fish intermingle with sunbaked, beachy colors in this exciting, Mexican-spiced spike-stitch design by Josi Hannon Madera.

KNITTED MEASUREMENTS
■ Approx 9"/23cm wide x 97"/246.5cm long

MATERIALS
■ 3 3½oz/100g balls (each approx 218yd/199m) of Knit One, Crochet Too *Parfait Solids* (wool) in #1460 golden rod (A) 🔳
■ 2 balls in #1369 soft pimento (C)
■ 1 ball in #1521 soft seafoam (B)
■ Size J/10 (6mm) crochet hook *or size to obtain gauge*

GAUGE
12 sts and 20 rows to 4"/10cm over spike st using size J/10 (6mm) crochet hook. *Take time to check gauge.*

Notes
1 Scarf is made of 2 strips.
2 Strips are worked lengthways, then joined together.
3 When changing colors, draw new color through last 2 lps on hook, then ch and turn.

STITCH GLOSSARY

Spike stitch (SP st) Working from front to back, insert hook into top of st of specified rows below. Yo and draw up a lp that is the same height as working row. Yo and draw through both lps on hook to complete st.

SP2 Work SP st in top of st 2 rows below.
SP3 Work SP st in top of st 3 rows below.
SP4 Work SP st in top of st 4 rows below.
SP5 Work SP st in top of st 5 rows below.
SP6 Work SP st in top of st 6 rows below.

STRIP I
With A, ch 290.
Row I Sc in 2nd ch from hook and in each ch across—289 sts. Ch 1, turn.
Rows 2–5 Sc in each st across. Ch 1, turn.
Row 6 Rep row 2, changing to B in last st. Ch 1, turn.
Row 7 Sc in first 2 sts, *SP2 over next st, SP3 over next st, SP4 over next st, SP5 over next st, SP6 over next st, SP5 over next st, SP4 over next st, SP3 over next st, SP2 over next st, sc in next 3 sts; rep from * 23 times more, ending last rep with sc in last 2 sts. Ch 1, turn.
Rows 8–11 Rep row 2.
Row 12 Rep row 2, changing to A in last st. Ch 1, turn.
Row 13 Sc in first st, *SP6 over next st,

SP5 over next st, SP4 over next st, SP3 over next st, SP2 over next st, sc in next st, SP2 over next st, SP3 over next st, SP4 over next st, SP5 over next st, SP6 over next st, sc in next st; rep from * across. Ch 1, turn.

Rows 14–17 Rep row 2.

Row 18 Rep row 2, changing to C in last st. Ch 1, turn.

Row 19 Sc in first st, *SP2 over next st, SP4 over next st, SP2 over next st, sc in next st; rep from * across. Ch 1, turn.

Rows 20 and 21 Rep row 2. Fasten off.

Work as for Strip I, but do not fasten off when row 21 is completed.

Joining

Place strips tog so WS are facing and rows 21 are even.

Row 1 Ch 1, sl st in last st worked of Strip II, *sl st in corresponding st of Strip I, sl st in next st of Strip II; rep from *, end sl st in corresponding st of Strip I. Fasten off.

Block scarf lightly to measurements.

Embroidery

With RS facing and C, embroider a row of blanket stitches (shown above right) around entire edge.

BLANKET STITCH

■■■■▶

A provocative art project disguised as a scarf, Gitta Schrade's pattern makes imaginative use of beads within a silky-soft design.

KNITTED MEASUREMENTS
■ Approx 8"/20.5cm wide x 61"/155cm long

MATERIALS
■ 2 1¾oz/50g balls (each approx 136yds/125m) of Naturally Yarns *Merino et Soie 8 Ply* (wool/silk) each in #214 brown (A) and #215 green (B)
■ 1 ball each in #213 navy (C), #216 goldenrod (D), #211 lilac (E), #207 red (F) and #212 teal (G) ⬛
■ Size E/4 (3.5mm) crochet hook *or size to obtain gauge*
■ Silver and gold safety pins
■ Forty 6mm glass beads in assorted colors

GAUGE
23 sts to 4"/10cm over sc using size E/4 (3.5mm) crochet hook.
Take time to check gauge.

Notes
1 Scarf is made of three strips that are stitched together.
2 Each strip is made in unjoined rounds.

STITCH GLOSSARY
Double treble crochet (dtr) Yo 3 times, insert hook into st, yo and draw up a lp, [yo and draw through 2 lps on hook] 4 times.

CENTER STRIP
With A, ch 300.
Rnd 1 Sc in 2nd ch from hook, sc in next 52 ch, dc in next 180 ch, sc in last 66 ch, mark last st made with the silver safety pin to indicate end of first half of rnd; ch 1, turn to bottom lps of foundation ch, sc in same ch as last sc, ch 1, sc in next 38 lps, dc in next 80 lps, tr in next 80 lps, dc in next 40 lps, sc in each rem st to end, ch 1, sc in same lp as last sc, mark last st made with the gold safety pin to indicate end of second half of rnd. You will be working in a spiral marking the last st made with the gold safety pin to indicate end of rnd.
Rnd 2 Ch 1, sc in first 40 sts, dc in next 10 sts, tr in next 50 sts, dc in next 10 sts, sc in next 25 sts, dc in next 15 sts, tr in next 40 sts, dc in next 10 sts, sc in next 12 sts, dc in next 6 sts, tr in next 6 sts, dc in next 5 sts, sc in each st to silver safety pin; turn to opposite side, ch 1, sc in same st as last sc, [ch 1, sc in next st] twice, sc in next 33 sts, dc in next 17 sts, sc in next 11 sts, dc in next 13 sts, tr in next 15 sts, dc in next 27 sts, tr in next 71 sts, dc in next 9 sts, sc

in next 20 sts, dc in next 10 sts, tr in next 7 sts, dc in next 2 sts, sc in each st to gold safety pin.

Rnd 3 Ch 1, sc in same st as last sc, [ch 1, sc in next st] twice, sc in next 36 sts, dc in next 30 sts, tr in next 13 sts, dtr in next 9 sts, tr in next 4 sts, dc in next 11 sts, sc in next 28 sts, dc in next 8 sts, tr in next 20 sts, dc in next 18 sts, sc in next 26 sts, dc in next 8 sts, tr in next 4 sts, dc in next 6 sts, sc in each st to silver safety pin; turn to opposite side, ch 1, sc in same st as last sc, [ch 1, sc in next st] 3 times, sc in next 34 sts, dc in next 6 sts, tr in next 6 sts, dtr in next 3 sts, tr in next 3 sts, dc in next 3 sts, sc in next 7 sts, dc in next 13 sts, tr in next 5 sts, dtr in next 4 sts, tr in next 4 sts, dc in next 5 sts, sc in next 21 sts, dc in next 4 sts, tr in next 13 sts, dtr in next 14 sts, tr in next 5 sts, dc in next 11 sts, sc in next 20 sts, dc in next 15 sts, sc in next 21 sts, dc in next 10 sts, tr in next 7 sts, dc in next 4 sts, sc in each st to gold safety pin, sl st in next st. Fasten off.

RIGHT STRIP

With B, ch 280.

Rnd 1 Sc in 2nd ch from hook, sc in next 50 ch, dc in next 160 ch, sc in last 69 ch, mark last st made with the silver safety pin to indicate end of first half of rnd; ch 1, turn to bottom lps of foundation ch, sc in same ch as last sc, ch 1, sc in next 38 lps, dc in next 25 lps, tr in next 10 lps, dtr in

next 8 lps, tr in next 7 lps, dc in next 30 lps, sc in next 40 lps, dc in next 12 lps, tr in next 9 lps, dc in next 10 lps, sc in each rem lp to end, mark last st made with the gold safety pin to indicate end of second half of rnd. You will be working in a spiral, marking the last st made with the gold safety pin to indicate end of rnd.

Rnd 2 Ch 1, sc in same st as last sc, [ch 1, sc in next st] twice, sc in next 45 sts, dc in next 8 sts, tr in next 9 sts, dc in next 7 sts, sc in next 13 sts, dc in next 6 sts, tr in next 20 sts, dc in next 14 sts, sc in next 40 sts, dc in next 7 sts, tr in next 6 sts, dc in next 6 sts, sc in each st to silver safety pin; turn to opposite side, ch 1, sc in same st as last sc, [ch 1, sc in next st] twice, sc in next 37 sts, dc in next 27 sts, tr in next 8 sts, dtr in next 9 sts, tr in next 3 sts, dc in next 32 sts, sc in next 43 sts, dc in next 11 sts, tr in next 6 sts, dc in next 9 sts, sc in each st to gold safety pin.

Rnd 3 Ch 1, sc in same st as last sc, [ch 1, sc in next st] 3 times, sc in next 43 sts, dc in next 9 sts, tr in next 9 sts, dc in next 7 sts, sc in next 18 sts, dc in next 10 sts, tr in next 10 sts, dc in next 7 sts, sc in next 44 sts, dc in next 10 sts, tr in next 10 sts, dc in next 10 sts, sc in each st to silver safety pin; turn to opposite side, ch 1, sc in same st as last sc, [ch 1, sc in next st] 3 times, sc in next 48 sts, dc in next 19 sts, tr in next 8 sts, dtr in next 5 sts, tr in next 4 sts, dc in next 30 sts, sc in next 49 sts, dc in next 24 sts, sc in next 22 sts, dc in next 4 sts, tr in next 8 sts, dc in next 7 sts, sc in each st to gold safety pin, sl st in next st. Fasten off.

LEFT STRIP

Work as for right strip using C.

SMALL 12-PETAL FLOWER

(make 5 pieces)

Center

With E, ch 5. Join ch with a sl st forming a ring.

Rnd 1 (RS) Ch 1, work 12 sc in ring, join rnd with a sl st in first sc. Fasten off.

Petals

With RS facing, join G with a sc in any st.

Rnd 2 Ch 5, sc in same st as joining, [work (sc, ch 5, sc) in next st] 11 times, join rnd with a sl st in first sc. Fasten off. Make 4 more flowers as foll: the first using F for center and G for petals, the second using G for center and D for petals, the third using D for both center and petals, and the fourth using E for both center and petals. (**Note** when making solid color flowers, do not fasten off after rnd 1 is completed.)

MEDIUM 12-PETAL FLOWER

(make 3 pieces)

Center

With A, ch 5. Join ch with a sl st forming a ring.

Rnd 1 (RS) Ch 1, work 12 sc in ring, join rnd with a sl st in first sc. Fasten off.

Petals

With RS facing, join E with a sc in any st.

Rnd 2 Ch 9, sc in same st as joining, [work (sc, ch 9, sc) in next st] 11 times, join rnd with a sl st in first sc. Fasten off. Make 2 more flowers as foll: the first using G for center and D for petals, and the second using F for both center and petals. (Note when making solid color flowers, do not fasten off after rnd 1 is completed.)

LARGE 7-PETAL FLOWER

(make 4 pieces)

Center

With E, ch 7. Join ch with a sl st forming a ring.

Rnd 1 (RS) Ch 3, work 14 dc in ring, join rnd with a sl st in first dc. Fasten off.

Petals

With RS facing, join C with a sl st in any st.

Rnd 2 [Ch 7, sc in 2nd ch from hook, dc in next 5 ch, sk next st, sl in next st] 7 times.

Fasten off. Make 3 more flowers as foll: the first using D for center and G for petals, and the second using D for center and E for petals, and the third using G for center and F for petals.

LARGE ROSE

(make 2 pieces)

First row of petals

With E, ch 7. Join ch with a sl st forming a ring.

Rnd 1 (RS) Ch 6 (counts as 1 tr and ch 2), [tr, ch 2] 7 times in ring, join rnd with a sl st in 4th ch of beg ch-5—8 ch-2 sps.

Rnd 2 [Work (dc, tr, dtr, tr, dc) in next ch-2 sp] 8 times, join rnd with a sl st in first dc.

Second row of petals

With RS facing, fold first row of petals towards you.

Rnd 3 On WS, [dc between next 2 dc of rnd 2, ch 3] 8 times, join rnd with a sl st in first dc—8 ch-3 sps.

Rnd 4 [Work (dc, 2 tr, dtr, 2 tr, dc) in next ch-3 sp] 8 times, join rnd with a sl st in first dc. Fasten off.

Center row of petals

With RS facing, and working over beg ring, join D with a sl st between any 2 tr of rnd 1.

Rnd 5 Work (dc, tr, dtr, tr, dc) in same sp as joining, sk next 2 tr, [work (dc, tr, dtr, tr, dc) between next 2 tr of rnd 1, sk next 2 tr] 3 times, join rnd with a sl st in first dc—4 petals made. Fasten off. Make one more flower using F for first and second rows of petals and C for center row of petals.

SMALL ROSE

(make 2 pieces)

Foll large rose instructions, make 1 using D for first row of petals and A for center row of petals, and one more using G for first row of petals and F for center row of petals.

EXTRA-LARGE 3-PETAL FLOWER

(make 2 pieces)

Center

With B, ch 7. Join ch with a sl st forming a ring.

Rnd 1 (RS) Ch 1, work 14 sc in ring, join rnd with a sl st in first sc. Fasten off.

Rnd 2 Ch 2, working in back lps only, [dc in next st, work 2 dc in next st] 7 times, join rnd with a sl st in first dc—21 sts. Fasten off.

Raised ridge

With RS facing, join D with a sc in any free lp of rnd 2.

Rnd 3 Work 1 more sc in same lp as joining, *work 2 sc in next free lp; rep from * around, join rnd with a sl st in first sc. Fasten off.

Petals

With RS facing, join A with a sc in any st of rnd 2.

Rnd 4 Work 1 more sc in same st as joining, work 2 dc in next st, work 2 tr in next 3 sts, work 2 dc in next st, work 2 sc in next st, [work 2 sc in next st, work 2 dc in next st, work 2 tr in next 3 sts, work 2 dc in next st, work 2 sc in next st] twice, join rnd with a sl st in first sc—3 petals made. Fasten off. With RS facing, join D with a sl st in same st as joining.

Rnd 5 Ch 1, [sc in next 2 sts, work 2 dc in next 10 sts, sc in next 2 sts] 3 times, join rnd with a sl st in first sc. Fasten off. Make one more flower using A for center, B for raised ridge, D for rnd 4 of petals and B for rnd 5.

(make 8 pieces)

With A, ch 15.

Rnd 1 (RS) Sc in 2nd ch from hook, sc in next ch, dc in next 2 ch, tr in next 2 ch, dtr in next ch, ch 5, sl st in next ch, ch 5, turn to bottom lps of foundation ch (unworked foundation ch forms stem), sk bottom lp opposite last sl st made, dtr in next lp, tr in next 2 lps, dc in next 2 lps, sc in last 2 lps. Fasten off. Make one more leave using A and 6 more using B.

(make 8 pieces)

With A, ch 17.

Rnd 1 (RS) Sc in 2nd ch from hook, sc in next 4 ch, dc in next 4 ch, tr in next ch, ch 4, sl st in next ch, ch 4, turn to bottom lps of foundation ch (unworked foundation ch forms stem), sk bottom lp opposite last sl st made, dtr in next 3 lps, tr in next 3 lps, dc in next 3 lps, sc in last 2 lps. Fasten off. Make one more leaf using A and 4 more using B.

Place strips side by side on work surface. Sew tog where edges meet, leaving approx 13"/33cm to 15"/38cm unstitched at each end for fringe. Arrange flowers and leaves as shown. Sew pieces in place using matching yarn color. Sew one bead to center of both sizes of 12-petal flowers and roses, and 3 beads to center of each large 7-petal flower; extra-large 3-petal flowers are not accented with beads. Use rem beads to accent some leaf veins and to decorate scarf.

FLORAL MOTIF SCARF

Flowers in the rain

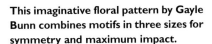

This imaginative floral pattern by Gayle Bunn combines motifs in three sizes for symmetry and maximum impact.

KNITTED MEASUREMENTS
- Approx 4½"/11.5cm wide x 48"/122cm long

MATERIALS
- 1 1¾oz/50g ball (each approx 136yd/125m) of Patons *Grace* (cotton) each in #60027 ginger (A), #60437 rose (B), #60603 apricot (C), #60416 blush (D) and #60604 terracotta (E) 🔳
- Size F/5 (3.75mm) crochet hook *or size to obtain gauge*

GAUGE
One small flower is 1½"/4cm across using size F/5 (3.75mm) crochet hook.
One medium flower is 2¼"/5.5cm across using size F/5 (3.75mm) crochet hook.
One large flower is 2¾"/7cm across using size F/5 (3.75mm) crochet hook.
Take time to check gauge.

STITCH GLOSSARY
Cluster st (CL) [Yo and draw up a loop, yo and draw through 2 loops on hook] 3 times in next sp (or st), yo and draw though all loops on hook.

Long single crochet (Lsc) Insert hook into top of st of specified rnd below. Yo and draw up a lp that is the same height as working rnd. Yo and draw through both lps on hook to complete st.

SMALL BASIC FLOWER
With first color, ch 4. Join ch with a sl st forming a ring.

Rnd 1 Ch 1, work 12 sc in ring, join rnd with a sl st in first st. Fasten off.

Rnd 2 Join second color with a sl st in any sc, ch 1, sc in same sp as joining, *ch 2, CL in next sc, ch 2, sc in next sc; rep from * around, end CL in last sc, ch 2, join rnd with a sl st in first sc. Fasten off.

SMALL FLOWER 1
(make 9 pieces)
Use A for first color and B for second color.

SMALL FLOWER 2
(make 9 pieces)
Use C for first color and D for second color.

MEDIUM BASIC FLOWER
With first, ch 4. Join ch with a sl st forming a ring.

Rnd 1 Ch 1, work 9 sc in ring, join rnd with a sl st to first sc.

Rnd 2 Ch 1, work 2 sc in each sc around, join rnd with a sl st in first sc—18 sc. Fasten off.

Rnd 3 Join second color with a sl st in any sc, ch 1, sc in same sp as joining, *ch 3, sk next 2 sc, sc in next sc; rep from * around, end ch 3, sk last 2 sc, join rnd with a sl st in first sc.

Rnd 4 Ch 1, sc in same sp as joining, *ch 2, work 2 dc in next ch-3 sp, ch 2, sc in next sc; rep from * around, end ch 2, join rnd with a sl st in first sc. Fasten off.

Rnd 5 Join third color with a sl st in sp between any 2 dc, ch 1, sc in same sp as joining, *ch 3, Lsc in next sc of rnd 2, ch 3, sc in sp between next 2 dc; rep from * around, end ch 3, join rnd with a sl st in first sc. Fasten off.

MEDIUM FLOWER I
(make 6 pieces)
Use A for first color, C for second color and E for third color.

MEDIUM FLOWER 2
(make 7 pieces)
Use C for first color, A for second color and B for third color.

LARGE BASIC FLOWER
With first color, ch 4. Join ch with a sl st forming a ring.

Rnd I Ch 4 (counts as dc and ch 1), [dc, ch 1] 7 times in ring, join rnd with a sl st in 3rd ch of beg ch-4. Fasten off.

Rnd 2 Join second color with a sl st in front lp of any dc, ch 1, sc in same sp as joining, *ch 2, work 2 dc in next ch-1 sp, ch 2, sc in front lp of next dc; rep from * around, end work 2 dc in last ch-1 sp, ch 2, join rnd with a sl st in first sc. Fasten off.

Rnd 3 Join third color with a sl st in free back lp of dc behind rnd 2, ch 1, sc in same lp as joining , *ch 4, sc in free back lp of next dc; rep from * around, end ch 4, join rnd with a sl st in first sc.

Rnd 4 Ch 1, sc in same sp as joining, *ch 2, work 4 dc in next ch-4 sp, ch 2, sc in next sc; rep from * around, end ch 2, join rnd with a sl st in first sc. Fasten off.

LARGE FLOWER I
(make 7 pieces)
Use A for first color, D for second color and C for third color.

LARGE FLOWER 2
(make 6 pieces)
Use E for first color, C for second color and A for third color.

FINISHING
Arrange flowers on work surface in a 4½"/11.5cm wide x 48"/122cm long strip having 2 flowers side by side, but never placing identical flowers together. Tack flowers together at points where they touch using matching yarn color.

OPENWORK DIAMOND SCARF

Byzan-tones

■■■◻

This **diamond scarf** by **Gayle Bunn** evokes the luxury of ancient times with its gently contrasting colors and vivid, recurrent motifs.

KNITTED MEASUREMENTS
■ Approx 6½"/16.5cm wide x 79"/200.5cm long

MATERIALS
■ 2 1¾oz/50g balls (each approx 181yd/165m) of Filatura di Crosa/ Tahki•Stacy Charles, Inc. *Zarina* (wool) in #1494 light grey (A) ■■
■ 1 ball each in #1462 light blue (B) and #1451 tan (C)
■ Size F/5 (3.75mm) crochet hook *or size to obtain gauge*

GAUGE
2 pat reps and 18 rows to 5"/12.5cm over pat st using size F/5 (3.75mm) crochet hook.
Take time to check gauge.

Notes
1 Scarf is worked lengthways.
2 When changing colors, draw new color through last 2 lps on hook.

SCARF

With A, ch 530.

Foundation row Sc in 2nd ch from hook, sc in next ch, *ch 5, sk next 6 ch, work (2 dc, ch 1, 2 dc) in next ch (shell made), ch 5, sk next 6 ch, sc in next 3 ch; rep from *, end last rep with sc in last 2 ch—33 pat reps. Turn.

Row 1 Ch 1, sc in first 2 sc, *ch 5, work shell in ch-1 sp of next shell, ch 5, sc in next 3 sc; rep from *, end last rep with sc in last 2 sc. Turn.

Row 2 Rep row 1, changing to B. Turn.

Row 3 With B, ch 3 (counts as 1 dc), dc in first sc, *ch 5, sk first dc of next shell, sc in next dc, sc in next ch-1 sp, sc in next dc, ch 5, work shell in center sc of next 3 sc group; rep from *, end last rep with 2 dc in last sc. Turn.

Row 4 Ch 3 (counts as 1 dc), dc in first dc, *ch 5, sc in next 3 sc, ch 5, shell in ch-1 sp of next shell; rep from *, end last rep with 2 dc in top of ch-3 t-ch. Turn.

Row 5 Rep row 4, changing to C. Turn.

Row 6 With C, ch 1, sc in first 2 sc, *ch 5, work shell in center sc of next 3 sc group, ch 5, sk first dc of next shell, sc in next dc, sc in next ch-1 sp, sc in next dc;

rep from *, end last rep with sc in last 2 dc. Turn.

Rows 7 and 8 Rep row 1, changing to A at end of row 8.

Row 9 Rep row 3.

Rows 10 and 11 Rep row 4, changing to C at end of row 11.

Rows 12–14 Rep rows 6–8, changing to B at end of row 14.

Row 15 Rep row 3.

Rows 16 and 17 Rep row 4, changing to A at end of row 17 .

Rows 18 and 19 Rep rows 6 and 7.

Row 20 Ch 1, sc in first 2 sc, *ch 6, sc in ch-1 sp of next shell, ch 6, sc in next 3 sc; rep from *, end last rep with sc in last 2 sc. Fasten off.

Block scarf lightly to measurements.

■■■■▶

Suzanne Atkinson offers an arresting design that mirrors the light-catching effect of stained glass.

KNITTED MEASUREMENTS
■ Approx 10"/25.5cm wide x 66"/167.5cm long

MATERIALS
■ 7 1¾oz/50g balls (each approx 54yd/49m) of Karabella Yarns *Aurora Bulky* (wool) in #14 eggplant (A) (**5**)
■ 4 balls in #910 lilac (B)
■ 3 balls in #7 light purple (C)
■ 2 balls in #9 light pink (D)
■ Size I/9 (5.5mm) crochet hook *or size to obtain gauge*

GAUGE
Motif 1 is 3⅜"/8.5cm square using size I/9 (5.5mm) crochet hook.
Take time to check gauge.

Notes

1 When changing colors at the end of a row, draw new color through 2 lps on hook to complete the last st.

2 When changing colors at the end of a row where there is a dec, draw new color through 3 lps on hook to complete the dec.

STITCH GLOSSARY

Double single crochet (dsc) Insert hook in next st and draw up a lp. Yo and draw through one lp on hook, yo and through rem 2 lps on hook.

dsc2tog [Insert hook into next st and draw up a lp, yo and draw through one lp on hook] twice, yo and draw through all 3 lps on hook.

MOTIF I
With A, ch 21.

Row 1 (RS) Dsc in 2nd ch from hook and in next 8 ch, sk next 2 ch, dsc in last 9 ch. Ch 1, turn.

Row 2 Dsc in first 8 sts, sk next 2 sts, dsc in last 8 sts changing to B in last st. Ch 1, turn.

Row 3 Dsc in first 7 sts, sk next 2 sts, dsc in last 7 sts. Ch 1, turn.

Row 4 Dsc in first 6 sts, sk next 2 sts, dsc in last 6 sts changing to C in last st. Ch 1, turn.

Row 5 Dsc in first 5 sts, sk next 2 sts, dsc in last 5 sts. Ch 1, turn.

Row 6 Dsc in first 4 sts, sk next 2 sts, dsc in last 4 sts changing to D in last st. Ch 1, turn.

Row 7 Dsc in first 3 sts, sk next 2 sts, dsc in last 3 sts. Ch 1, turn.

Row 8 Dsc in first 2 sts, sk next 2 sts, dsc in last 2 sts. Ch 1, turn.

Row 9 Dsc in first st, sk next 2 sts, dsc in last st. Fasten off.

MOTIF 2

With A, ch 10.

Row 1 (RS) Work dsc in 2nd ch from hook and in each ch across. With RS facing, work 9 dsc evenly spaced across top right edge of motif 1. Ch 1, turn. Beg with row 2, cont to work as for motif 1. Fasten off.

MOTIF 3

With A, ch 9; fasten off and set aside. With RS facing, join A with sl st in end of row 9 of motif 1.

Row 1 (RS) Work 9 dsc evenly spaced across top left edge of motif 1, then dsc in each ch of reserved ch. Ch 1, turn. Beg with row 2, cont to work as for motif 1. Fasten off.

MOTIF 4

With RS facing, join A with a sl st in end of row 1 of motif 2.

Row 1 (RS) Work 9 dsc evenly spaced across top right edge of motif 2. Ch 1, turn.

Row 2 Dsc in first 7 sts, dsc2tog changing to B. Ch 1, turn.

Row 3 Dsc2tog, dsc in last 6 sts. Ch 1, turn.

Row 4 Dsc in first 5 sts, dsc2tog changing to C. Ch 1, turn.

Row 5 Dsc2tog, dsc in last 4 sts. Ch 1, turn.

Row 6 Dsc in first 3 sts, dsc2tog changing to D. Ch 1, turn.

Row 7 Dsc2tog, dsc in last 2 sts. Ch 1, turn.

Row 8 Dsc in first st, dsc2tog. Ch 1, turn.

Row 9 Dsc2tog. Fasten off.

MOTIF 5

With RS facing, join A with a sl st in end of row 9 of motif 2.

Row 1 (RS) Work 9 dsc evenly spaced across top left edge of motif 2, then work 9 dsc evenly spaced across top right edge of motif 3. Ch 1, turn. Beg with row 2, cont to work as for motif 1. Fasten off.

MOTIF 6

With right side facing, join A with a sl st in end of row 9 of motif 3.

Row 1 (RS) Work 9 dsc evenly spaced across top left edge of motif 3. Ch 1, turn.

Row 2 Dsc2tog, dsc in last 7 sts changing to B in last st. Ch 1, turn.

Row 3 Dsc in first 6 sts, dsc2tog. Ch 1, turn.

Row 4 Dsc2tog, dsc in last 5 sts changing to C in last st. Ch 1, turn.

Row 5 Dsc in first 4 sts, dsc2tog. Ch 1, turn.

Row 6 Dsc2tog, dsc in last 3 sts changing to D in last st. Ch 1, turn.

Row 7 Dsc in first 2 sts, dsc2tog. Ch 1, turn.

Row 8 Dsc2tog, dsc in last st. Ch 1, turn.

Row 7 Dsc2tog. Fasten off.

MOTIF 7

With RS facing, join A with a sl st in end of row 9 of motif 4.

Row 1 (RS) Work 9 dsc evenly spaced across top left edge of motif 4, then work 9 dsc evenly spaced across top right edge of motif 5. Ch 1, turn. Beg with row 2, cont to work as for motif 1. Fasten off.

MOTIF 8

With RS facing, join A with a sl st in end of row 9 of motif 5.

Row 1 (RS) Work 9 dsc evenly spaced across top left edge of motif 5, then work 9 dsc evenly spaced across top right edge of motif 6. Ch 1, turn. Beg with row 2, cont to work as for motif 1. Fasten off. Referring to placement diagram, rep motifs 4–8 12 times more, then motif 5 only to form point at opposite end of scarf—69 motifs completed.

FINISHING

Block scarf lightly to measurements.

Edging

With RS facing, join A with a sl st in bottom corner of motif 1. **Rnd 1** Ch 1, making sure that work lies flat, sc evenly around entire edge working 2 sc in each corner and 3 sc in each point, join rnd with a sl st in first sc. **Rnd 2** Ch 1, working from left to right, sc in each st around, join rnd with a sl st in first sc. Fasten off.

STRIPED LACE SCARF

Marsh madness

This light and airy mohair scarf by Christine L. Walter attracts attention with its mysterious, muted earth tones.

KNITTED MEASUREMENTS
■ Approx 8"/20cm wide x 64"/162.5cm long (excluding fringe)

MATERIALS
■ 3 1¾oz/50g balls (each approx 136yd/124m) of Reynolds/JCA Yarns *Fusion* (mohair/acrylic/wool) in #8 marsh (**5**)
■ Size I/9 (5.5mm) crochet hook *or size to obtain gauge*

GAUGE
14 sts and 6 rows to 4"/10cm over shell st pat using size I/9 (5.5mm) crochet hook. *Take time to check gauge.*

SCARF
Ch 31.
Row 1 Work 4 dc in 4th ch from hook, sk next 4 ch, hdc in next ch, *ch 2, sk next ch, dc in next ch, ch 1, sk next ch, dc in next ch, ch 1, sk next ch, work 5 dc in next ch (shell made), sk next 4 ch, hdc in next ch; rep from * once more. Ch 3, turn.

Row 2 Work 4 dc in first hdc, hdc in 5th dc of first shell, *ch 2, dc in next dc, ch 1, dc in next dc, ch 1, work 5 dc in next hdc, hdc in 5th dc of next shell; rep from * once more, ending rep with hdc in 3rd ch of ch-3 t-ch of last shell. Ch 3, turn. Rep row 2 for shell st pat until piece measures 64"/162.5cm from beg. Fasten off.

FINISHING
Block scarf lightly to measurements.

FRINGE
Cut 14"/33cm strands of yarn. Using 4 strands for each fringe, attach 13 fringes evenly spaced across each end of scarf. Trim ends evenly.

■■■▢

A mix of medallions atop an open mesh pattern, this striking design by Karen J. Hay is a breath of fresh air in any season.

KNITTED MEASUREMENTS
■ Approx 4"/10cm wide x 70"/179cm long

MATERIALS
■ 3 1¾oz/50g balls (each approx 137yd/125m) of Plymouth Yarn *Wildflower DK* (cotton/acrylic) in #157 light teal (MC) **3**
■ 1 ball in #55 dark teal (CC)
■ Size F/5 (3.75mm) crochet hook *or size to obtain gauge*

GAUGE
4 ch-6 sps and 9 rows to 4"/10cm over trellis pat using size F/5 (3.75mm) crochet hook.
One small flower is 3"/7.5cm across using size F/5 (3.75mm) crochet hook.
One large flower is 4"/10cm across using size F/5 (3.75mm) crochet hook.
Take time to check gauge.

Note
When changing colors from one rnd to the next, draw new color through sl st as you join the rnd.

STITCH GLOSSARY
Starting ring Make a slip knot 5"/12.5cm from tail end of yarn. Place slip knot on hook. To form starting ring, loosely wrap tail of yarn counter-clockwise around index finger of hand holding crochet hook. Slide ring off finger and work first round of sts into starting ring. After working the first round, pull gently on the yarn tail to close ring.

Long single crochet (Lsc) Insert hook into top of st of rnd below. Yo and draw up a lp that is the same height as working rnd. Yo and draw through both lps on hook to complete st.

SCARF
With MC, ch 22.

Row 1 Work (dc, ch 2, 2 dc) in 4th ch from hook, ch 2, sk next 2 ch, sc in next ch, *ch 6, sk next 3 ch, sc in next ch; rep from * twice more, ch 2, sk next 2 ch, work (2 dc, ch 2, 2 dc) in last ch (shell made). Ch 1, turn.

Row 2 Sk first dc, sl st in next dc and ch-2 sp, ch 3 (counts as 1 dc), work (dc, ch 2, 2 dc) in same ch-2 sp as sl st (beg shell made), ch 4, sk ch-2 sp, sc in next ch-6 sp, *ch 6, sc in next ch-6 sp; rep from * once more, ch 4, sk ch-2 sp, work shell in ch-2 sp of shell. Ch 1, turn.

Row 3 Sk first dc, sl st in next dc and ch-

2 sp, ch 3 (counts as 1 dc), work beg shell in same ch-2 sp as sl st, ch 2, sc in next ch-4 sp, *ch 6, sc in next ch-sp; rep from * twice more, ch 2, work shell in last ch-2 sp. Ch 1, turn. Rep rows 2 and 3 for trellis pat until piece measures 70"/179cm from beg (slightly stretched), end on row 3. Ch 1, turn.

Top edging

Row 1 Sk first dc, sl st in next dc and ch-2 sp, ch 3, work beg shell in same ch-2 sp as sl st, sk ch-2 sp, tr in next sc, *work shell in next ch-6 sp, tr in next sc; rep from * twice more, work shell in ch-2 sp of last shell. Ch 3, turn.

Row 2 Work 6 dc in ch-2 sp of first shell, *sc in next tr, work 6 dc in ch-2 sp of next shell; rep from * 3 times more, ch 3, join ch with a sl st in 3rd ch of ch-3 t-ch of row below. Fasten off.

Bottom edging

Turn piece so RS is facing and bottom lps of foundation ch are at top. Join yarn with a sl st in bottom lp of first shell.

Row 1 Ch 3, work beg shell in same lp as joining, tr in bottom lp of next sc, *work shell in base of next ch-3 sp, tr in bottom lp of next sc; rep from * twice more, work shell in bottom lp of last shell. Ch 3, turn.

Row 2 Rep row 2 as for top edging. Fasten off.

SMALL BASIC FLOWER

Make starting ring.

Rnd 1 (RS) Ch 1, work 8 sc in ring, join rnd with a sl st in first st—8 sts.

First row of petals

Rnd 2 Ch 1, sc in first st, *ch 3, sc in next sc; rep from * around 6 times more, end ch 3, join rnd with a sl st in first st—8 ch-3 sps.

Rnd 3 Ch 1, *work (sc, hdc, 2 dc, hdc, sc) in next ch-3 sp; rep from * around, join rnd with a sl st in first st—8 petals (48 sts). Fasten off.

Second row of petals

Rnd 4 With RS facing, fold first row of petals towards you. Join yarn with a sl st between any 2 sts of rnd 3, ch 4, *sk next 4 sts, sc between next 2 sts, ch 4; rep from * around, join rnd with a sl st in beg sl st—12 ch-4 sps.

Rnd 5 Ch 1, work (sc, hdc, dc, 2 tr, dc, hdc, sc) in each ch-4 sp around, join rnd with a sl st in first st—12 petals. Fasten off.

FLOWER 1

(make 3 pieces)

Work rnds 1 and 2 using CC, rnds 3 and 4 using MC and rnd 5 using CC.

FLOWER 2

(make 2 pieces)

Work rnds 1 and 2 using MC, rnds 3 and

4 using CC and rnd 5 using MC.

Make starting ring.

Rnd 1 Ch 1, work 8 sc in ring, join rnd with a sl st in first st—8 sts.

Rnd 2 Ch 1, work 2 sc in each st around, join rnd with a sl st in first st—16 sts.

Rnd 3 Ch 1, work 2 sc in first st, Lsc over next st, [work 2 sc in next st, Lsc over next st] 7 times, join rnd with a sl st in first st—24 sts.

Rnd 4 Ch 1, work 2 Lsc over first st, sc in next 2 sts, [work 2 Lsc over next st, sc in next 2 sts] 7 times, join rnd with a sl st in first st—32 sts.

First row of petals

Rnd 5 Ch 3, sk first 2 sts, *sc in next st, sk next 2 sts, ch 3; rep from * around, join rnd with a sl st in first ch of beg ch-3—11 ch-3 sps.

Rnd 6 Ch 1, *work (sc, hdc, 2 dc, hdc, sc) in next ch-3 sp; rep from * around, join rnd with a sl st in first st—11 petals. Fasten off.

Second row of petals

Rnd 7 With RS facing, fold first row of petals towards you. Join yarn with a sl st between any 2 dc of rnd 6, ch 4, *sc between 2 dc of next petal, ch 4; rep from * around, join with sl st in first sc—11 ch-3 sps.

Rnd 8 Ch 1, work (sc, hdc, dc, 2 tr, dc, hdc, sc) in each ch-4 lp around, join rnd with a sl st in first st—11 petals. Fasten off.

FLOWER 3
Work rnds 1–5 using CC, rnds 6 and 7 using MC and rnd 8 using CC.

FLOWER 4
Work rnds 1–4 using CC, rnds 5–7 using MC and rnd 8 using CC.

FLOWER 5
Work rnds 1–5 using MC, rnds 6 and 7 using CC and rnd 8 using MC.

FLOWER 6
Work rnds 1 and 2 using MC, rnd 3 using CC, rnds 4 and 5 using MC, rnds 6 and 7 using CC and rnd 8 using MC.

FLOWER 7
Work rnds 1 and 2 using CC, rnd 3 using MC, rnds 4 and 5 using CC, rnds 6 and 7 using MC and rnd 8 using CC.

FINISHING
Block scarf lightly to measurements. Referring to photo on page 78, arrange flowers on scarf, then sew in place.

I heart crochet

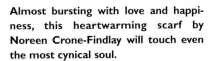

Almost bursting with love and happiness, this heartwarming scarf by Noreen Crone-Findlay will touch even the most cynical soul.

KNITTED MEASUREMENTS
- Approx 5"/12.5cm wide x 42"/106.5cm long

MATERIALS
- 1 4.4oz/125g ball (each approx 250yd/230m) of S.R. Kertzer *Super 10* (cotton) in #3533 daffodil (A), #3871 cobalt (B), #3764 kelly green (C) and #3997 frankly scarlet (D) (4)
- Size G/6 (4mm) crochet hook or size to obtain gauge

GAUGE
One doll is 3½"/9cm across and 4½"/11.5cm tall using size G/6 (4mm) crochet hook.
Take time to check gauge.

BASIC DOLL IN DRESS

Head

With A, ch 3. Join ch with a sl st forming a ring.

Rnd I Ch 1, work 6 sc in ring, join rnd with a sl st in first sc.

Rnd 2 Ch 1, work 2 sc in each st around, join rnd with a sl st in first sc—12 sc. Ch 1, turn.

Neck

Row I Sc in first 2 sts. Ch 1, turn.

Row 2 Sc in each of 2 sts. Ch 10, turn.

First arm

Row 3 Hdc in 6th ch from hook, hdc in next 4 ch, sc in next 2 sts. Ch 10, turn.

Second arm

Row 4 Hdc in 6th ch from hook, hdc in next 4 ch, join with a sl st in side edge of row 2. Fasten off.

HAIR

With RS of head facing, join yarn with a sl st in first st above right side edge of neck.

Row I Sc in same st as joining, [ch 5, sc in next sc] 9 times. Fasten off.

DRESS

Row I Ch 7 for right shoulder strap. Join ch with a sl st forming a ring. With RS of doll facing, slip ring onto doll's right arm. Sc in each of 2 center sts between arms, ch 7 for left shoulder strap, turn, wrap ch around left arm, join ch with a sl st in first ch forming a ring. Ch 1, turn.

Row 2 Work, 2 sc in each sc—4 sc. Ch 1, turn.

Rows 3–9 Work 2 sc in first st, sc in each st across. Ch 1, turn.

Row 10 Sc in each of 11 sts. Fasten off.

Dolls I and 5

Use A for head, neck and arms. Use B for hair and dress.

Doll 3

Use A for head, neck and arms. Use C for hair and B for dress.

Doll 7

Use A for head, neck and arms. Use B for hair and C for dress.

Doll 9

Use A for head, neck and arms. Use C for hair and dress.

BASIC DOLL IN OVERALLS

Work as for doll in dress until hair is completed.

Overalls

Rep rows 2 and 3 as for dress.

Row 3 Sc in each st across. Ch 1, turn.

First leg

Row 4 Sc in first 2 sts. Ch 1, turn.

Rows 5–8 Sc in each of 2 sts. Ch 1, turn.

Row 9 Rep row 5. Ch 5 for toe loop, turn.

Row 10 Rep row 5. Ch 1, turn to inside edge of leg, then sl st in each row to crotch. Fasten off.

Second leg

Row 4 Join yarn with a sl st in next st after first leg, ch 1, sc in same st as joining, sc in last st. Ch 1, turn.

Rows 5–9 Sc in each of 2 sts. Ch 1, turn.

Row 10 Rep row 5. Ch 5 for toe loop, turn to inside edge of leg, then sl st in each row to crotch. Fasten off.

Doll 2

Use A for head, neck and arms. Use C for hair and overalls.

Doll 4

Use A for head, neck and arms. Use B for hair and C for overalls.

Doll 6

Use A for head, neck and arms. Use C for hair and B for overalls.

Dolls 8 and 10

Use A for head, neck and arms. Use B for hair and overalls.

JOIN DOLLS WITH HEARTS

Working from right to left, place dolls 1 through 10 on work surface.

Row I (RS) With D, make a slip knot. Place dolls 1 and tog WS tog. Insert hook through t-ch of right arm of doll 1 and t-ch of left arm of doll 2. Place slip knot on hook. Draw lp of slip knot through, yo and draw through lp, then sc in same sp as joining. Ch 1, turn.

Row 2 Work 2 sc in sc. Ch 1, turn.

Row 3 Work 2 sc in each st—4 sc. Ch 1, turn.

Row 4 Work 2 sc in first st, sc in next 2 sts, work 2 sc in last st, join with a sl st in 2nd hair loop of doll 2—6 sc. Ch 1, turn.

Row 5 Work 2 sc in first st, sc in next 4 sts, work 2 sc in last st, join with a sl st in 2nd hair loop of doll 1—8 sc. Ch 1, turn.

Row 6 Sk first st, work 5 dc in next st, sk next st, sl st in next st, sk next st, work 5 dc in next st, sk next st, sl st in last st. Fasten off. Working in this manner, cont to join doll 2 to doll 3, doll 3 to doll 4, etc.

Block scarf lightly to measurements.

Grass

Turn scarf so RS is facing and bottom edge is at top. Join C with a sl st in t-ch of right arm of doll 10. **Row 1** Ch 9, sc in ch-5 toe loop of doll, *sc in next 2 ch of toe loop, sc in next 2 sc of leg, ch 3, sc in next 2 sc of next leg, sc in next 2 ch of next toe loop, ch 3, sc in next 11 sts of next doll, ch 3; rep from * across, ch 9, join with a sl st in t-ch of left arm of doll 1. Ch 2, turn. **Row 2** Work 12 hdc in first ch-9 sp, hdc in each sc and ch to opposite ch-9 sp, end work 12 hdc in 2nd ch-9 sp, drawing B through all 3 lps on hook to complete last hdc.

Sky

Row 1 Ch 3, dc in 2nd hair loop of doll 1, ch 9, *sc in 5th hair loop, ch 7, sc in 3rd dc of first shoulder of heart, ch 5, sc in 2nd shoulder of heart, ch 7; rep* across, end ch 9, dc in 2nd hair loop of doll 10, ch 4, join with a sl st in first C hdc. Ch 1, turn. **Row 2** Work 5 sc in first ch-4 sp, sc in next dc, work 11 hdc in next ch-9 sp, *hdc in next sc, work 7 hdc in next ch-7 sp, hdc in next sc, work 5 hdc in next ch-5 sp, hdc in next sc, work 7 hdc in next ch-7 sp; * rep from across, end hdc in last sc, work 11 hdc in last ch-9 sp, sc in last dc, work 5 sc in last ch-4 sp. Fasten off.

Center heart

With RS facing, locate 2 center sts on short end of scarf. Join D with a sl in first of these 2 sts. **Row 1** Sc in same st as joining, sc in next st. Ch 1, turn. **Row 2** Sc in each of 2 sts. Ch 1, turn. **Row 3** Work 2 sc in each st—4 sc. Ch 1, turn. **Row 4** Work 2 sc in first st, sc in next 2 sts, work 2 sc in last st—6 sc. Ch 1, turn. **Row 5** Work 2 sc in first st, sc in next 4 sts, work 2 sc in last st—8 sc. Turn. **Row 6** Sk first st, work 5 dc in next st, sk next st, sl st in next st, sk next st, work 5 dc in next st, sk next st, sl st in last st. Fasten off.

Second heart

With RS facing, sk 6 sts to the right of center heart. Join D with a sl st in the 7th st. Rep rows 1–5 as for center heart. Turn. **Row 6** Sl st in first dc of shoulder of center heart, sk first st of second heart, work 5 dc in next st, sk next st, sl st in next st, sk next st, work 5 dc in next st, sk next st, sl st in last st. Fasten off.

Third heart

With RS facing, sk 5 sts to the left of center heart. Join D with a sl st in next st. Cont to work as for second heart to row 6. **Row 6** Sk first st, work 5 dc in next st, sk next st, sl st in next st, sk next st, work 5 dc in next st, sk next st, sl st in last st, then sl st in first dc of shoulder of center heart. Fasten off. Rep heart trim at opposite end of scarf.

Coral imperative

Whether employed as a scarf or a wrap, this bright shell design by Lisa Gentry will have all eyes on you.

KNITTED MEASUREMENTS

■ Approx 9"/23cm wide x 58"/147.5cm long (excluding fringe)

MATERIALS

■ 3 3½oz/100g skeins (each approx 124yd/114m) of Moda Dea/Coats & Clark *Metro* (acrylic/nylon) in #9664 sunset (5)

■ Size L/11 (8mm) crochet hook *or size to obtain gauge*

GAUGE

One whole shell is 9½"/24cm across and 5"/12.5cm high using size L/11 (8mm) crochet hook.

Take time to check gauge.

Note

To join yarn with a sc, make a slip knot and place on hook. Insert hook into st (or row) and draw up a lp, yo and draw through 2 lps on hook.

STITCH GLOSSARY

sc2tog [Insert hook into next st and draw up a lp] twice, yo and draw through all 3 lps on hook.

WHOLE SHELL

(make 6 pieces)

Ch 26. Work in back lps only throughout.

Row 1 (WS) Sc in 2nd ch from hook and in each ch across—25 sts. Ch 1, turn.

Rows 2–5 Sc in each st across. Ch 1, turn. When row 5 is completed, ch 3, turn.

Row 6 (RS) Dc in first st, *ch 1, sk next st, dc in next st; rep from * across. Ch 1, turn.

Row 7 Sc in each dc and ch-1 sp across—25 sts. Ch 1, turn.

Row 8 Rep row 2. Ch 1, turn.

Row 9 *Sk next st, sc in next st; rep from *, end sc in last st—13 sts. Ch 4, turn.

Row 10 Sk first st, dc in next st, *ch 1, sk next st, dc in next st; rep from * across, end dc in last st. Ch 1, turn.

Row 11 Rep row 7—13 sts. Ch 1, turn.

Row 12 Rep row 9—7 sts. Ch 1, turn.

Row 13 Rep row 9—4 sts. Ch 1, turn.

Row 14 [Sc2tog] twice. Fasten off.

JOINING WHOLE SHELLS

Referring to placement diagram, arrange 6 whole shells side by side on work surface for shells 1–6. To join shell 7 to shells 1 and 2, work as foll: with WS of shell 1 facing, join yarn with a sc in last row, then work 11 more sc evenly spaced along LH edge to first row, ch 1, with WS of shell 2 facing, sc in first row at RH edge, then work 11 more sc evenly spaced to last row. Ch 1, turn.

Row 2 (RS) Working through back lps only, sc in each st and ch across—25 sts. Ch 1, turn. Cont to work as for whole shell beg with row 3. Working in the same manner, cont to join shell 8 to shells 2 and 3, shell 9 to shells 3 and 4, shell 10 to shells 4 and 5, and shell 11 to shells 5 and 6.

JOINING HALF SHELLS AT SIDE EDGES

Refer to placement diagram on page 92. To join half shell 12 to shell 1, work as foll: With WS of shell 1 facing, join yarn with a sc in first row at RH edge, then work 12 more sc evenly spaced to last row—13 sts. Ch 1, turn. Working through back lps only, cont as foll:

Rows 2–5 Sc in each st across. Ch 1, turn. When row 5 is completed, ch 4 (counts as 1 dc and ch 1) turn.

Row 6 (RS) Dc in first st, *ch 1, sk next st, dc in next st; rep from * across. Ch 1, turn.

Row 7 Sc in each dc and ch-1 sp across—13 sts. Ch 1, turn.

Row 8 Rep row 2. Ch 1, turn.

Row 9 *Sk next st, sc in next st; rep from *, end sc in last st—7 sts. Ch 4, turn.

Row 10 Sk first st, dc in next st, *ch 1, sk next st, dc in next st; rep from * across, end dc in last st. Ch 1, turn.

Row 11 Rep row 7—7 sts. Ch 1, turn.

Row 12 Rep row 9—4 sts. Ch 1, turn.

Row 13 [Sk next st, sc in next st] twice—2 sts. Ch 1, turn.

Row 14 Sc2tog. Fasten off. To join half shell 13 to shell 6, work as foll: With WS of shell 6 facing, join yarn with a sc in last row at LH edge, then work 12 more sc evenly spaced to first row—13 sts. Ch 1, turn. Working through back lps only, rep rows 2–14. Fasten off.

JOINING HALF SHELLS ALONG TOP EDGE

Refer to placement diagram. To join half shell 14 to half shell 12 and whole shell 7, work as foll: with WS of shell 12 facing, join yarn with a sc in last row, then work 11 more sc evenly spaced along LH edge to first row, sc in top of shell 1, with WS of shell 7 facing, sc in first row at RH edge, then work 11 more sc evenly spaced to last row—25 sts. Ch 1, turn. Working through back lps only, cont as foll:

Row 2 (RS) Sc in each st across. Ch 1, turn.

Row 3 Sc in first 9 sts, [sk next st, sc in next st] 4 times, sc in last 8 sts—21 sts. Ch 1, turn.

Row 4 Sc in first 7 sts, [sk next st, sc in next st] 4 times, sc in last 6 sts—17 sts. Ch 1, turn.

Row 5 Sc in first 5 sts, [sk next st, sc in next st] 4 times, sc in last 4 sts—13 sts. Ch 1, turn.

Row 6 Sc in first st, sk next st, sc in next st, sk next st, hdc in next 2 sts, dc in next st, hdc in next 2 sts, sk next st, sc in next st, sk next st, sc in last st—9 sts. Fasten off. Working in the same manner, cont to join shell 15 to shells 7 and 8, shell 16 to shells 8 and 9, shell 17 to shells 9 and 10, shell 18 to shells 10 and 11, and shell 19 to shells 11 and 13.

FINISHING

Edging

With RS facing, join yarn with a sc in left top corner. **Rnd 1** Making sure that work lies flat, sc evenly along side edge to bottom edge. Working through bottom lps of foundation ch, sc in each lp across bottom edge. Ch 1, turn to side edge. Sc evenly along side edge to top edge. Ch 3, working through both lps, dc in each st across top edge, ch 3, join rnd with a sl st in first sc. Fasten off.

Fringe

Cut 20"/51cm strands of yarn. Using one strand for each fringe, attach 18 fringes evenly spaced across each end of scarf. Trim ends at varying lengths as desired.

Pompoms

Make 9 pompoms 1½"/4cm in diameter. Sew one between each whole shell across bottom edge. On each side edge, sew one pompom to first fringe and one to last fringe.

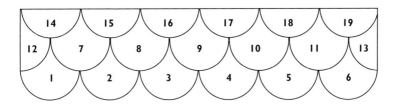

NOTES

NOTES

RESOURCES

US RESOURCES

Write to the yarn companies listed below for purchasing and mail-order information.

Alchemy Yarns of Transformation
P.O. Box 1080
Sebastopol, CA 95473
www.alchemyyarns.com

Anny Blatt
7796 Boardwalk
Brighton, MI 48116
www.annyblatt.com

Berroco, Inc.
P.O. Box 367
14 Elmdale Road
Uxbridge, MA 01569
www.berroco.com

Caron International
200 West 3rd Street
Washington, NC 27889
www.caron.com

Classic Elite Yarns
122 Western Avenue
Lowell, MA 01851
www.classiceliteyarns.com

Coats & Clark
Two LakePointe Plaza
4135 South Stream Blvd.
Charlotte, NC 28217
www.coatsandclark.com

Dale of Norway, Inc.
4750 Shelburne Rd.
Shelburne, VT 05482
www.daleofnorway.com

Fiber Trends
315 Colorado Park Place
P.O. Box 7266
East Wenatchee, WA 98802
www.fibertrends.com

Fiesta Yarns
5401 San Diego NE
Albuquerque, NM 87113
www.fiestayarns.com

Filatura Di Crosa
distributed by
Tahki •Stacy Charles, Inc.

GGH
distributed by
Muench Yarns

JCA
35 Scales Lane
Townsend, MA 01469
www.jcacrafts.com

JAEGER
distributed by
Westmnster Fibers, Inc.

Karabella Yarns
1201 Broadway
New York, NY 10001
www.karabellayarns.com

Knit One, Crochet Too, Inc.
91 Tandberg Trail, Unit 6
Windham, ME 04062
www.knitonecrochettoo.com

Lion Brand Yarn
34 West 15th Street
New York, NY 10011
www.lionbrand.com

Moda Dea
distributed by
Coats & Clark
www.modadea.com

Muench Yarns, Inc.
1323 Scott Street
Petaluma, CA 94954
www.myyarn.com

Naturally
distributed by
Fiber Trends
www.naturallyyarnsnz.com

Plymouth Yarn Company
P.O. Box 28
Bristol, PA 19007
www.plymouthyarn.com

Reynolds
distributed by
JCA

Rowan Yarns
distributed by
Westmnster Fibers, Inc.

South West Trading Company
918 South Park Lane
Suite 102
Tempe, AZ 85281
www.soysilk.com

Tahki•Stacy Charles, Inc.
70-30 80th Street
Building #36
Ridgewood, NY 11385
www.tahkistacycharles.com

Tahki Yarns
distributed by
Tahki•Stacy Charles, Inc.

Trendsetter Yarns
16745 Saticoy Street
Suite 101
Van Nuys, CA 91406
www.trendsetteryarns.com

Westminster Fibers
4 Townsend West, Unit 8
Nashua, NH 03063
www.westminsterfibers.com

Canadian Resources

*Write to US resources for
mail-order availability
of yarns not listed.*

S.R. Kertzer, Ltd.
50 Trowers Road
Woodbridge, ON
Canada L4L 7K6
www.kertzer.com

**The Old Mill Knitting
Company, Inc.**
F.G. P.O. Box 81176
Ancaster, Ontario L9G 4X2
www.oldmillknitting.com

Patons Yarns
320 Livingstone Avenue
South
Listowel, ON
Canada N4W 3H3
www.patonsyarns.com

UK RESOURCES

*Not all yarns used in this
book are available in
the UK. For yarns not
available, make a
comparable substitute or
contact the US manufac-
turer for purchasing and
mail-order information.*

Rowan
Green Lane Mill
Holmfirth
HD9 2DX England
www.knitrowan.com

VOGUE KNITTING CROCHETED SCARVES TWO

Editorial Director
TRISHA MALCOLM

Art Director
CHI LING MOY

Executive Editor
CARLA S. SCOTT

Book Division Manager
ERICA SMITH

Graphic Designer
SHEENA T. PAUL

Associate Editor
ERIN WALSH

Yarn Editor
TANIS GRAY

Instructions Editor
PAT HARSTE

Instructions Proofreader
RITA GREENFEDER

Production Manager
DAVID JOINNIDES

Photography
JACK DEUTSCH STUDIO

Photo Stylist
LAURA MAFFEO

Copywriter
ALAN YOUNG

Copy Editor
WENDY R. PRESTON

■

President,
Sixth&Spring Books
ART JOINNIDES